THE EVOLUTION OF OIL CONCESSIONS IN
THE MIDDLE EAST
AND
NORTH AFRICA

The
Evolution of Oil Concessions
in the
Middle East and North Africa

by

Henry Cattan

Licencié en Droit (Paris)

LL.M. (London)

Foreword by
Fred A. Davies

Published for the
PARKER SCHOOL OF FOREIGN
AND COMPARATIVE LAW

1967

Oceana Publications, Inc.

Dobbs Ferry, New York

CONTENTS

FOREWORD

Henry Cattan was born, and received his early education, in Jerusalem, Palestine. He studied law at the Universities of Paris and London, receiving degrees from each, and later taught law at the Jerusalem Law School. He has been engaged in the active practice and teaching of law for some 35 years and has long been recognized as one of the distinguished lawyers of the Middle East.

In the course of his practice, Mr. Cattan has counseled on oil and pipeline matters for the last 20 years. His knowledge of common law, civil law and Islamic law contributed to his unique value in assisting in the settlement of concessionary problems and in the adjustment to new conditions and concepts. It was in his capacity as legal advisor and consultant to Arabian American Oil Company and Trans-Arabian Pipe Line Company that I first came to know him.

In this book, Mr. Cattan has succeeded in encompassing in a concise and authoritative manner the pertinent features of oil concessions and the changes which have taken place in such agreements since the beginnings of the oil industry in the Middle East and North Africa.

I first arrived in the Middle East in 1930. Having lived with and under the terms of oil concessions for the next thirty years, I can well testify to the value and importance of Mr. Cattan's book. A concession agreement—or an economic development contract as it might well be called—is the charter for oil operations in the Middle East and many other areas. It establishes the rights and obligations of the parties. This is not to say that the provisions of oil concessions are immutable. Mr. Cattan's tracing of the evolution of such agreements demonstrates how they have been adapted to changing circumstances by agreement of the parties. Respect by the parties for their agreements has encouraged the oil companies to dedicate their investments and efforts to the discovery and development of oil in many countries throughout the Middle East and North Africa. Daily production in those countries in 1966 amounted to some 12,000,000 barrels—almost half the output of the Free World.

vii

Mr. Cattan's book gives, for the first time, a complete analysis of the provisions of oil concession agreements and traces their adjustment in the light of changing times, conditions and concepts. It will, I venture to hope, contribute to a better understanding of oil concessions and the problems involved in the relationships between Governments and oil companies. It will, I believe, be included in the library of all those interested in the development of oil and other resources in the Middle East and North Africa.

Fred A. Davies
Former Chairman of the
Board of Directors
Arabian American Oil Company

Lafayette, California
January 3, 1967

PREFACE

The history of oil concessions in the Middle East and North Africa is intricately interwoven with the political, economic and social developments of the area. Although such developments are of great interest, they do not fall within the scope of this work which is essentially concerned with the evolution of oil concessions and the comparative analysis of their juridical and financial conditions.[1]

The scope of this work is limited in three respects:

First, it is restricted geographically to the consideration of oil concessions in the Middle East and North Africa.

Secondly, early concessions that never became operative either by lapse or otherwise, or never led to the discovery and production of oil, have almost generally been ignored.

Thirdly, the nature of this study did not permit consideration of pipeline concessions.

The development of the oil industry in the Middle East is of comparatively recent date. Petroleum gas, bitumen and naphtha were not completely unknown in early times but their uses were limited. Petroleum gas was the source of the "Eternal Fires" worshipped in Mesopotamia; bitumen served the Egyptians for the preparation of mummies[2] and naphtha was used by the Greeks in the preparation of weapons. Nowadays, a thousand and one uses are made of petroleum and its derivatives.

It was not until a little more than half a century ago that the first major oil discovery in the Middle East was made at Masjid-i-Sulaiman in Persia (1908). This was followed by the major oil discoveries made at Kirkuk in Iraq (1927), at Bahrain (1932), in Saudi Arabia (1938),

---

[1] For the purposes of this study, the writer has consulted the text of most oil concessions in the Middle East and North Africa. Some may be found in specialized books and publications while the most recent concessions have been published in *Petroleum Legislation*, *Platt's Oilgram* and *The Middle East Economic Survey*. Others are not generally available.

[2] *Oil in the Middle East*, 1964, Petroleum Information Bureau, London, p. 3.

in Kuwait (1938) and in Qatar (1939). Since then further discoveries were made in the same and other countries in the Middle East.[3]

The picture of oil discovery in North Africa, though not so spectacular, is nonetheless dramatic. Small quantities of oil had been found as early as 1909 in Egypt, 1934 in Morocco and later in Algeria, but it was not until after mid-century that major oil discoveries were made in the Algerian Sahara in 1956 and in Libya in 1957. Excluding minor discoveries, the development of oil production in the African continent is hardly ten years old. The largest oil producers in order of importance in Africa in 1964 were Libya, Algeria, Egypt and Nigeria.

At present, Kuwait, Saudi Arabia, Iran and Iraq rank among the seven largest oil producing countries in the world, closely and rapidly followed by Libya, while Abu Dhabi, Algeria, Bahrain, Egypt and Qatar can also be regarded as major oil producing countries.

In a relatively short time oil production in Arab countries acquired world importance. The Middle East alone today accounts for over one-fourth (27.5%) of world oil production and possesses almost two-thirds (61%) of the world's proven oil reserves.[4] The combined crude oil production of the Middle East and North Africa exceeds one-third of world production.[5] The oil production of Kuwait for 1964 was about three times the production of the whole of Europe during the same year.[6] Libya during the same year produced more oil than Europe. At the end of 1963 it was estimated that the proven reserves of Saudi Arabia were greater than those of the United States.[7] The Middle East has always played and still plays an important role in human destiny: it is not only the cradle of history and civilization and the birthplace of the three great monotheistic religions, it is now the oil reservoir of the world.

The world of today, its industries, airplanes, ships, railways, homes and factories depend on oil. The legal instrument which has enabled

---

[3] Oil was also discovered in the Neutral Zone in 1953, in Syria in 1956, in Abu Dhabi in 1958 and in Oman in 1964. Production in Syria and Oman has not commenced as yet pending the construction of pipelines to the coasts.

[4] See Appendix II-E.

[5] See Appendices II-A and II-E.

[6] The production of Kuwait reached 106,390,000 tons in 1964 while during the same year Western Europe produced 20,660,000 tons and Eastern Europe produced 15,870,000 tons: Petroleum Information Bureau, London.

[7] *Oil in the Middle East,* op. cit., p. 8.

the development of this tremendous industry was the oil concession. This does not mean that the concession system is the only form of oil exploitation. There exist today in the Middle East and North Africa three systems of oil exploitation:

(1) the concession system which is the oldest and, until recent times, the most widespread;

(2) the concession system coupled with a participation or joint venture arrangement in favour of the State;

(3) the system of direct exploitation by the producing country.

Because of the risks inherent in oil exploration and the large investment required, the last of those three systems is the least generalized. The main features of the other two systems will be examined in the following pages.

By reason of the industrial, economic and strategic value of petroleum, the international personality of the State as one of the contracting parties and the vicissitudes—economic, social and political—supervening during its life, the oil concession surpasses all other contractual arrangements in magnitude, originality and complexity. Few, if any, contracts have ever had the importance of the oil concession agreement.

The oil concession is a species of long term contract which has to reconcile two apparently conflicting needs: stability and evolution. Those two needs are, in fact, two interdependent conditions in an oil concession.

The need for stability arises from the importance of oil concessions to the parties concerned, namely, the producing countries whose revenue, economic development and social progress sometimes largely depend upon their oil income and production;[8] the oil companies whose capital, resources and skill are committed to the promotion and advancement of the oil industry; the consuming countries whose industry and economic life are related to a large extent to their sources of supply of crude oil and refined products.

Stability, however, does not exclude evolution. The need for evolution arises from the nature of the oil concession which is necessarily concluded for a long period. In this respect, an oil concession

---

[8] Appendix II-D shows the extent of dependence of certain producing countries on their oil revenue.

differs from a contract whose performance requires no appreciable lapse of time. Contracts whose execution is spread over a long term of years and particularly oil agreements may become subject to many influences and cannot, therefore, escape an unavoidable evolutionary process. The early period of the oil industry in the Middle East was characterized by a static pattern of contractual relationships between the oil companies and the producing countries. In contrast, the present period is marked by changes in ideas and concepts which have led to radical variations in the oil concession system.

The evolution in oil concessions has been both legal and financial.

The legal evolution is of some significance. The oil concession has advanced that branch of the law relating to State contracts with individuals and corporations. Although the law of State contracts and oil concessions is a chapter whose pages have not yet been completely written, recent concessions have contributed to the development of legal doctrine concerning long term contractual arrangements to which the State is a party. This aspect is considered in a separate study.[9]

The financial evolution of oil concessions is no less striking. The main evolution here has been from a cash payment per ton of oil to Government participation in the profits of the enterprise. As a result, the financial structure of concessions has undergone drastic change. This evolution should not be regarded only as a financial adjustment in the relationship between the parties which has resulted in a mere increase of concession payments. Such evolution had a deeper effect and significance. It is evident that this development has constructively converted oil concessions into contractual arrangements between the producing countries and the oil companies in which each party makes its contribution—the producing countries contributing the natural resource and certain facilities and the oil companies contributing the capital, knowledge and markets—with the profits of the enterprise being equally or substantially shared between them. The concept of mutual benefit is much more marked and underlined in the modern formula of profit sharing or in the joint venture arrangements now existing in certain cases between the oil company and the producing country than in the old State-concessionaire relationship based almost exclusively on the royalty. There is no doubt that the concept of mu-

---

[9] See *The Law of Oil Concessions in the Middle East and North Africa* by the author.

tual benefit tends to increase the mutual goodwill and understanding between the parties.

This sense of mutual goodwill and understanding has made it possible for the parties in most cases to solve their evolutionary problems and conflicts of interest in an orderly manner. The study of the evolution of oil concessions is not only of academic interest: knowledge of the past may serve as guidance for the future.

A large measure of the credit for this work must be attributed to my friend, Mr. William L. Owen, General Counsel of Arabian American Oil Company, who has suggested its need and whose advice and assistance have been invaluable. I wish also to express my deep gratitude to Mr. Douglas Erskine and the late Mr. Louis E. Goodyear of Dhahran for their helpful suggestions, to Mr. Edmund Burke, Jr. of New York for his assistance, to Mr. D. Marquardt and Mr. F. Mefferd of Tripoli, Libya, for their comments on the Libyan law, and to Me. J. Loyrette, Me. J. Godard and Mr. V. Bremme, Director of *Pétrole Informations* of Paris, for providing me with some documentation relative to the North African concessions.

H. C.

Beirut, January 1, 1967

ABBREVIATIONS

AGIP	Assienda Generale Italiana Petroli
AIOC	Anglo-Iranian Oil Company
AJIL	The American Journal of International Law
Aminoil	American Independent Oil Company
Aramco	Arabian American Oil Company
Auxirap	Société Auxiliaire de la Régie Autonome des Pétroles
Bapco	Bahrain Petroleum Company
BRP	Bureau de Recherches de Pétrole
Consortium	Consortium of various oil companies with which Iran made its Agreement of September 20, 1954
EGPC	Egyptian General Petroleum Corporation
ENI	Ente Nazionale Idrocarburi
ERAP	Entreprise de Recherches et D'Activités Pètroliéres
Getty	Getty Oil Company
ICLQ	The International and Comparative Law Quarterly
IPC	Iraq Petroleum Company
KOC	Kuwait Oil Company
Neutral Zone	Saudi Arabia-Kuwait Neutral Zone
NIOC	National Iranian Oil Company
OPEC	Organization of Petroleum Exporting Countries
Pan American	With reference to the U.A.R., means Pan American U.A.R. Oil Company;

xv

With reference to Iran, means Pan American Petroleum Corporation;

With reference to Hadramaut, means Pan American Hadramaut Oil Company,

all being operating subsidiaries of Pan American International Oil Corporation whose name was changed in 1962 to American International Oil Company.

Petromin	General Petroleum and Mineral Organization of Saudi Arabia
Phillips	Phillips Petroleum Company
RAP	Régie Autonome des Pétroles
Sapphire	Sapphire Petroleum Ltd.
Shell	With reference to Kuwait, means Kuwait Shell Petroleum Development Company, Ltd.
Trapal	Société pour le Transport des Hydrocarbures Sahariens au Littoral Algérien
U.A.R.	United Arab Republic

Chapter I

Historical Review

The review of the evolution of oil concessions in the Middle East and North Africa may be divided into two periods:

1. The period prior to 1950;
2. The period since 1950.

The subdivision into the two periods mentioned is certainly not the only possible approach, but it does correspond to the historical evolution of oil concessions.[1] In fact, as will be seen later, the year 1950 was the turning point in the financial evolution of oil concessions in the Middle East.

SECTION I. CONDITIONS PRIOR TO 1950

Oil history in the Middle East began with the grant in 1901 by the Persian Government of an oil concession to W. K. D'Arcy. It was the first effective concession that resulted in the discovery and production of oil in the region. This concession was taken over by the Anglo-Persian Oil Company, subsequently named Anglo-Iranian Oil Company (AIOC), and was replaced by a new concession in 1933.

The D'Arcy concession was followed by a number of other concessions. The principal early concessions that led to the discovery and production of oil were the following:

— The concession to IPC in Iraq in 1925, followed in 1932 by the grant of a concession to British Oil Development Company

---

[1] For an historical survey of oil concessions in the Middle East, see in particular Longrigg, *Oil in the Middle East*, 2nd ed.; Shwadran, *The Middle East, Oil and the Great Powers 1959*, 2nd ed.; and Lenczowski, *Oil and State in the Middle East*. Regarding Kuwait, in particular, see *The Oil of Kuwait* by Samir Shamma (in Arabic).

1

(B.O.D.), later acquired by the Mosul Petroleum Company and further followed in 1938 by the grant of a concession to the Basrah Petroleum Company, both companies being affiliates of IPC;

— The concession to Standard Oil Company of California in Saudi Arabia in 1933, subsequently assigned to Aramco;
— The concession to KOC in Kuwait in 1934;
— The concession to Bapco in Bahrain in 1934;[2]
— The concession to Anglo-Persian Oil Company in Qatar in 1935;
— The concessions by Kuwait to Aminoil in 1948 and by Saudi Arabia to Pacific Western Oil Corporation (subsequently Getty) in 1949, both in the Neutral Zone.

With the exception of the last two concessions to Aminoil and Getty, oil concessions granted during the first half of the century almost generally followed the same pattern and embodied the same standard conditions. Their similarity was equalled only by their simplicity.

The concession agreements defined the grant, the area and the duration of the concession, the payments to be made by the concessionaire and, mostly in general terms, the mutual rights and obligations of the parties. Where the law of the country required it, they were ratified by a law or a decree. In most cases, the agreements were described as concessions, though sometimes they were designated as conventions, contracts or leases.

The grant made to the concessionaire was usually that of an exclusive right to search for, obtain, exploit, develop, render suitable for trade, carry away, export and sell petroleum and related substances.

The area was very large and if it did not include the whole territory of the conceding State, it covered its largest part. The D'Arcy concession extended to the whole of the Persian Empire (Article 1) with the exception of five provinces (Article 6) and covered an area

---

[2] Although Bapco's concession was granted on December 29, 1934, oil had previously been discovered in Bahrain by Bapco, a subsidiary of the Standard Oil Company of California, in the year 1932. Bapco then operated in Bahrain under the terms of an option for oil rights originally held by the Eastern and General Syndicate and subsequently assigned to the Standard Oil Company of California.

of 480,000 square miles. The area was reduced to 100,000 square miles in the new concession granted to AIOC in 1933 in replacement of the D'Arcy concession. IPC's concession (1925) was for the whole of Iraq east of the Tigris River, to the exclusion of the province of Basra and the "Transferred Territories" (Article 3).[3] The concession originally granted by Saudi Arabia to Standard Oil Company of California, subsequently assigned to Aramco, covered an area of approximately 371,000 square miles and was further extended in 1939 to about 496,000 square miles. The concession granted to KOC covered the area of Kuwait. The concession for Bahrain (1934) was limited to 100,000 acres, but subsequently extended to include all of the Sheikh's present and future dominions. The area of the concession granted to the Anglo-Persian Oil Company in Qatar (1935) extended to the whole country.

The duration of concessions was quite long and usually ranged between 60 to 75 years. The original D'Arcy concession was made for 60 years. Concessions of the IPC group in Iraq were granted for 75 years. Aramco's original concession in Saudi Arabia was made for 60 years but was subsequently extended to 66 years. The concession to KOC was for 75 years but was subsequently extended to 92 years. The concession in Bahrain (1934) was originally for 55 years, and subsequently extended to 90 years. The concession granted by Qatar to the Petroleum Development Company (1935) was for 75 years. The same period was stipulated in the agreement made in 1937 between the Sultan of Muscat and Oman and Petroleum Concessions Ltd. Both Aminoil's concession from Kuwait (1948) and Getty's concession from Saudi Arabia (1949) in the Neutral Zone were made for 60 years.

Judged by today's values, the financial terms of the earlier concessions seem modest. Although some concessions made provision for rents or tax commutation payments or fringe benefits, such as loans or the supply of petroleum, or exceptionally, as we shall see later, for some form of profit sharing, the principal financial feature of the oil concession was the royalty. The royalty was generally fixed at four

---

[3] The "Transferred Territories" were a strip transferred by Persia to Turkey in 1913 which later came under the sovereignty of Iraq. Such strip remained subject to the Anglo-Persian concession. This concession was subsequently taken over by a subsidiary of the Anglo-Persian Oil Company named the Khanaqin Oil Company.

shillings gold[4] or three rupees per ton of crude oil. Without attempting to develop precise figures for revenue, costs or profits for the early period of oil concessions which would obviously vary as to time and country, it can be said that four shillings gold per ton, when compared with the then existing prices of crude oil, constituted at the time a considerably more valuable consideration than that which it seems to represent today.

Summarizing the conditions obtaining prior to 1950, one can say that the period from 1901 to 1950 was characterized by:

(1) the large areas and long periods of oil concessions;

(2) the small number of operating companies;

(3) the relative uniformity and simplicity of concession terms;

(4) the royalty concept which constituted the principal financial basis of oil concessions;

(5) the comparative moderateness of the financial terms of concessions which was a consequence of the lower value of, and lesser demand for, crude oil during that early period;

(6) the slow evolution in the terms and conditions of concessionary agreements which was tantamount to stagnation and rigidity.

A wind of change began to blow during and immediately following the second World War when, in consequence of the fixing of the value of gold at $35.00 an ounce and the rapidly ascending prices of crude oil, the old royalty rate of four shillings gold per ton ceased to represent as substantial a consideration in favour of the producing country as it had in the past. The concessions granted to Aminoil and Getty in the Neutral Zone in 1948 and 1949 accordingly raised the old established royalty rate and envisaged substantial bonus payments and profit arrangements in favour of the Governments concerned.

SECTION 2. MAJOR DEVELOPMENTS SINCE 1950

It was at mid-century that the tide turned. The uniform pattern that had hitherto characterized oil concessions is now broken by a

---

[4] The value of four shillings gold at U.S. $35.00 the ounce amounted to U.S. $1.65.

succession of significant developments which resulted in a rapid evolution in their terms.

The factors underlying such evolution were numerous: the impact of certain new legal and economic concepts; the progress in oil technology; the discovery of the considerable oil reserves of the Middle East; the increase in world demand and consumption of oil and the dependence of Western Europe on Middle East oil. The concurrence of all such economic, legal and scientific factors revolutionized the relationships between producing countries and oil companies and gave a tremendous impetus to oil production which reached unparalleled figures. Daily oil production soared from one and a half million barrels in 1949 to over ten million barrels in 1965[5] while payments to the producing countries which stood at slightly over one hundred million dollars per annum in 1949 have now exceeded two billion dollars a year.[6]

Another significant result of such developments was the increase in the number of oil companies engaged in the exploration and production of oil. In early days, oil companies interested in securing concessions in the Middle East were not numerous. Large capital was required; the financial risks were enormous; the chances of oil discovery were not always promising; oil itself was not in great demand, especially at the beginning of the century when coal was considered the prime source of energy. It is not, therefore, surprising that few companies, except the major companies, showed interest during those days in securing oil concessions. It is evident that the major oil companies by their discoveries in Iran, Iraq, Kuwait, Saudi Arabia, Algeria and Libya, not only generally established the existence of oil in those regions but substantially reduced the elements of risk and speculation in oil exploration. These discoveries, coupled with the opening of submarine areas for oil exploitation and the freeing of large areas as a result of relinquishment, made it possible for newcomers and smaller companies to enter the oil business.

No attempt will be made here to examine all the developments which have occurred since mid-century in the oil industry. Many of these will be eventually or incidentally noted. However, we have selected for review or mention at this point some of the major de-

---

[5] Appendix II-A.
[6] Appendix II-C.

velopments which have influenced the course of the evolution of oil concessions and which we summarize as follows:

 A. The equal sharing of oil profits.

 B. The relinquishment concept.

 C. Government participation in the oil industry.

 D. The grant of offshore concessions in territorial waters and the continental shelf.

 E. The enactment of petroleum legislation.

 F. The establishment of national and international agencies concerned with the oil industry.

These developments will be concisely examined hereinafter.

A. THE EQUAL SHARING OF OIL PROFITS

In early days, as already remarked, the producing country's participation in the financial benefits of oil production was usually limited to the royalty and some other minor advantages. Though there existed instances of profit sharing in oil production between producing countries and concessionary companies, they were few and of not great consequence.[7] Such profit sharing assumed two forms: either a share in dividends distributed by the concessionaire or a share in the concessionaire's net profits.

The only instance of the former type was that found in AIOC's concession (1933). This form of profit sharing will be referred to in the discussion of royalties related to both tonnage and dividends in Section 4 of Chapter II.

Two instances of the latter form of profit sharing were found in early days in Persia and in Iraq.[8] Both can be traced to the D'Arcy concession (1901.) Article 10 of this concession provided that the concessionaire shall pay annually to the Persian Government a sum equal to 16% of the annual net profits of any company or companies formed for the exploitation of the concession. The similar provision

---

 [7] Instances of profit sharing arrangements in other types of concessions were also rare. Under the Suez Canal concession, the Egyptian Government was entitled to 15% of the concessionary company's profits: La Pradelle et Politis, *Recueil des Arbitrages Internationaux,* Vol. II, p. 344.

 [8] The abortive concessionary agreement made between Persia and the Sinclair Exploration Company on December 20, 1923 included a profit sharing provision rising progressively from 20% to 28% on the basis of the percentage of profits in relation to invested capital (Article XII).

found in Iraq was an offshoot of the D'Arcy concession and was included in the concession granted by Iraq to the Anglo-Persian Oil
Company with respect to the "Transferred Territories". These territories—transferred by Persia to Turkey in 1913 which subsequently
came under the sovereignty of Iraq—were subject to the concession
previously granted by Persia to D'Arcy in 1901. By an agreement
made on August 30, 1925 between Iraq and the Anglo-Persian Oil
Company, the Government recognized the company's right to exploit
the concession granted in the said "Transferred Territories" to D'Arcy
in 1901, subject to the same terms and conditions, including the right
to receive 16% of the annual net profits of the company. This concession was taken over by a subsidiary of the Anglo-Persian Oil Company, called the Khanaqin Oil Company.

The fate which those two profit sharing provisions encountered
in Iraq and Persia is worthy of consideration.

In Iraq, it appears that the Government was not satisfied with the
profit sharing arrangement. Consequently, the financial provisions of
the aforementioned agreement dated August 30, 1925 were altered
by a subsequent agreement made on May 24, 1926. The latter agreement recited in its preamble that the Iraqi Government is entitled
under the terms of the concession to 16% of the net profits of the
company to be ascertained in the manner set out in the agreement
dated August 30, 1925; however, the Government and the company
agreed that, in consideration of an extension of the period of the
concession, the company will pay to the Government a royalty dependent on the quantity of substances produced instead of a share of
its profits. Accordingly, the company undertook to pay to the Government a royalty per ton of the substances won and saved, subject
to deduction of water, foreign substances and oil used in company operations, at the rate of four shillings gold; after 20 years and
for each period of 10 years the royalty was to be increased or decreased in accordance with a formula related to the difference between
average market price and cost.

In Persia, the same profit sharing provision written in the D'Arcy
concession of 1901 was preserved, but its application gave rise to
certain difficulties between the Government and the Anglo-Persian
Oil Company (subsequently named AIOC). The Persian Government maintained that it had a right to share in the profits of all com-

panies dealing with oil extracted under the concession, whether or
not such companies operated in Persia. The company, however, maintained that the Government's right to 16% of the annual net profits
concerned only such companies as operated in Persia under the direct
organization of the D'Arcy concession. The issue was settled by an
agreement signed on December 22, 1920. The agreement provided
that the Persian Government was entitled to receive 16% of all net
profits arising from the mining, refining and marketing of Persian
oil, whether all the stages of the above processes were handled by the
company itself or through subsidiary companies in Persia or outside.
The Government, however, was not entitled to share in the profits
arising from the transportation of oil by means of ships. The agreement further specified the methods for ascertaining the profits of
refining and distributing companies handling oil and oil products in
addition to oil produced under the concession and provided that in
determining net profits, no deductions were to be made for interest
or dividends.[9] This profit sharing arrangement was eventually abandoned in the new concession granted in 1933 in replacement of the
D'Arcy concession in favour of a provision which reserved for Persia
a share in the dividends distributed by the concessionaire above a
certain level.[10]

It is remarkable that the only two provisions for the sharing of
oil profits which existed in early concessions were abandoned by the
parties by reason of differences over their implementation in favour
of fixed royalties in the one case and in favour of a percentage of dividends in the other case.

Two concessions granted shortly before mid-century with respect
to the Neutral Zone restored the concept—originally introduced but
subsequently abandoned in Persia—of the producing country's participation in the profits of the oil enterprise. Kuwait's concession to
Aminoil (1948) provided in Article 3 that 15% of the shares of a
subsidiary company to be organized by the concessionaire for exploring and exploiting the Neutral Zone shall be attributed to the
Sheikh without any financial contribution on his part: such arrangement amounted to giving the producing country an interest of 15%

---

[9] Shwadran, *The Middle East, Oil and the Great Powers 1959*, 2nd ed.,
pp. 35-37.

[10] See Section 4 of Chapter II.

in the enterprise and a 15% share in its profits. A year later, Saudi Arabia's parallel concession to Pacific Western Oil Corporation (subsequently Getty) in the Neutral Zone made provision for a profit sharing arrangement between the parties. Article 7 of the agreement stipulated that, in addition to the royalty, the Government will be entitled to 25% of the net profits realized from the sale of products[11] or by-products obtained by the company from the Neutral Zone and not refined by the company at any refinery built by the company in the Neutral Zone. It was further provided that the share of the Government in such profits shall be in the nature of a "carried interest", that is, the amount thereof shall be determined after the deduction of all charges properly allocable thereto, but no liability for the amount of any of such charges or any loss shall attach to the Government. It is assumed that this provision is equivalent to a profit sharing arrangement contingent upon payout, i.e., the recovery by the concessionaire of his investment.

However, it was the year 1950 that marked the turning point in the financial evolution of oil concessions. In that year Saudi Arabia and Aramco concluded the now famous agreement of December 30, 1950 which introduced in the Middle East[12] the concept of equal profit sharing between a producing country and the concessionaire.[13] By this agreement Saudi Arabia and Aramco revised the arrangement existing between them—which by reason of the passage of time and the increase in the value of oil in relation to gold had become an unequal economic bargain—in favour of the principle of equal sharing of profits. The change involved two major consequences. First, the concessionaire's payments to the producing country were associated with profits in addition to the fixed amounts previously payable per

---

[11] In the context used, the term "products" has been interpreted to include crude oil.

[12] The equal sharing of oil profits between the producing country and oil companies was first adopted in Venezuela in 1948.

[13] E. H. Brown has suggested that although the Saudi Arab Tax Decree was never applied to Getty, yet the Government's revenue from Getty probably amounts to more than the 50-50 principle applied by the law: *The Saudi Arabia Neutral Zone*, p. 102. S. H. Longrigg mentions that a profit sharing scheme had been examined by Anglo-Iranian and the Persian Government in 1948-49 but concedes that the equal profit sharing arrangement reached between the Saudi Arabian Government and Aramco was now agreed to and published for the first time: *Oil in the Middle East*, 2nd ed., p. 210.

unit of production and, secondly, the parties adopted the concept of the equal sharing of profits or equivalence of contractual advantages between them.

The concept of equal profit sharing replaced the royalty as the principal financial feature of oil concessions, though royalties have remained as a "floor" to the revenue of the conceding State, unaffected by the level of profits. In terms of income to Governments, the implementation of the 50-50 division of net profits meant approximately a threefold to a fourfold increase in the revenue previously afforded by the standard royalty rate of four shillings gold per ton.[14]

The introduction of the equal profit sharing concept in the concession agreement between Saudi Arabia and Aramco revolutionized the then existing level of payments by the oil concessionaire and had its impact on all other concessions, old or new alike. Usually the principle was implemented either in the form of a 50% income tax on profits (calculated before deduction of the royalty) against which the royalty was creditable, so that the income tax was the difference between 50% of this profit and the royalty, or by a straight division of profits between the oil concessionaire and the producing country. The principle found its way into the concession agreements in Kuwait, Iraq, Qatar and Bahrain and was adopted in new concessions granted, and in oil legislation promulgated, in Libya, Iran, Algeria, Tunisia, Morocco and the U.A.R. All existing concessions were thus revised by mutual agreement between the parties, but in one case a break occurred. This happened between AIOC and Iran in 1951. Although negotiations for revision of the 1933 concession had proceeded between the parties since 1948, no final agreement was reached and Iran nationalized the oil industry and vested AIOC's assets in a national company.[15]

The equal profit sharing concept has since undergone an evolution, one might even say the concept has suffered some erosion. In its practical application today, the concept varies to some extent from

---

[14] Four shillings gold per ton are equivalent to U.S. $0.22 cents per barrel approximately.

[15] The issues which arose between the parties as a result of such action, including the question of compensation, were settled on the occasion, and in consideration, of the agreement reached between Iran and the Consortium in 1954.

its formulation in 1950. In some new concessions deviations have even occurred. All these aspects will be examined in Sections 5 and 7 of the following Chapter.

B. The Relinquishment Concept

The concept of the gradual relinquishment by the concessionaire of unexploited portions of the concession area is another major development of recent times.

Relinquishment was unknown in the early oil concessions. The concessions granted by Iran, Kuwait, Bahrain and Qatar made no reference to relinquishment. The concession granted by Iraq in 1925 to the Turkish Petroleum Company (subsequently named IPC) envisaged in Article 6 a program of relinquishment on a small scale as follows: the Government reserved the right to select annually after four years from the date of the concession not less than 24 plots, each of an area of eight square miles, which it would offer for lease by means of tender to the public on the same terms and conditions as those provided in the concession. This provision for gradual relinquishment was, however, deleted by Article 5 of the revised concession granted to IPC in 1931.

Aramco's concession (1933) envisaged relinquishment. Article 9 of the concession required the company to relinquish to the Government such portions of the concession area as the company may decide not to explore or prospect further or to use otherwise in connection with the enterprise. By an agreement made on October 10, 1948 the parties agreed on a program for the relinquishment in stages of portions of the concession area amounting to a total of 198,000 square miles spread over a period of 22 years. Areas totalling 144,000 square miles were relinquished by 1963 under that agreement and on March 24, 1963 another arrangement was reached between the parties whereby the company agreed to a program of accelerated relinquishment entailing the immediate surrender of such portions of its concession area in excess of 125,000 square miles. The same agreement further embodied the company's undertaking to relinquish within six successive intervals of five years certain other portions so that, within 30 years after the date of the said agreement, the area to be retained by the company will measure not more than

20,000 square miles, i.e., about 4% of its original concession area.

Aramco's original concession of May 29, 1933 and its agreement with Saudi Arabia of October 10, 1948 which implemented the concept of the gradual relinquishment of oil concession areas were probably as significant and momentous as the agreement of December 30, 1950 between the same parties which introduced the equal profit sharing concept.

Since then the principle of relinquishment has been incorporated in petroleum legislation as well as in new and old concessions. The Libyan Petroleum Law (1955), as amended in 1961, required the progressive reduction of the concession area to 75% of the original area within five years from the date of the concession, to 50% within eight years from the same date, and to one-third or one-fourth of the original size (depending upon the zone in which the concession is located) within ten years from the date of the concession (Article 10). All Libyan concessions have incorporated these provisions. The Iranian Petroleum Act required the return within a maximum period of 10 years of half of the total surface area covered by the agreement (Article 10). This obligation was embodied in all Iranian oil agreements.

All new concessions have included a relinquishment obligation as a matter of course. The agreement made between Saudi Arabia and Japan Petroleum Trading Company required the company to relinquish on the third anniversary of the discovery of oil in commercial quantities, and every five years thereafter, 20% of the Government's one-half interest in the unexploited area. A similar provision was included in the agreement made between Kuwait and Arabian Oil Company. The same relinquishment provision was included in Saudi Arabia's agreement with Auxirap. The Kuwait-Shell agreement embodied the same principle and required the company on the third anniversary of discovery of oil in commercial quantities, and at the expiration of every five years thereafter, to relinquish to the Emir an area or areas to be selected by it and which will be equal in aggregate to 20% of the unexploited area at the date of relinquishment. The agreement between Mecom and Jordan (1964) provided for relinquishment of one-half of the concession area at the end of two years from the effective date of the concession and for further relinquishments at the end of each five-year period thereafter of 20% of the unexploited area.

The relinquishment concept also permeated to old concessions. Thus, in 1961 Qatar Petroleum Company relinquished one-third of its concession area. In 1963, Kuwait reached agreement with KOC to reduce the original area of the concession by about one half and also agreed upon a further reduction of the area to take effect prior to May 1967. In Iraq, the Government's negotiations with IPC broke down in 1961 on certain issues among which was the failure of the parties to agree on a mutually satisfactory relinquishment program. Thereupon Iraq enacted Law No. 80 of 1961 which imposed upon IPC what has been described as an "involuntary relinquishment": its effect was to reduce the area of the concessions held by the IPC group of companies to the actual portions under exploitation, i.e., to less than 1% of the original area and to relieve the released portions from all rights which the IPC group of companies held in such portions. Law No. 80 has been in issue between IPC and Iraq since 1961. Reasoning *ex post facto,* one may wonder whether the discard in 1931 of the relinquishment provisions embodied in the original IPC concession of 1925 may not have been a mistake.

The practice in North Africa with regard to relinquishment differs fundamentally from that followed in the Middle East: relinquishment applies to the search permit but not to the concession itself. Under the Sahara Petroleum Code, for example, the applicant is not granted a concession, but only an exclusive search permit, called "permit H", valid for five years (Articles 1-5). This permit can be renewed twice for maximum periods of five years each. The relinquishment obligation applies to the renewals of the search permit: on the occasion of the first renewal the area of the permit is reduced by one half, and on its second renewal the remaining area is reduced by one quarter (Article 8). The holder of the permit is entitled to the grant of a concession upon an exploitable discovery of oil within its area (Article 23). The grant of the concession entails the cancellation of the permit with respect to the area covered by the concession, but the permit subsists and remains operative outside the area of the concession granted to the holder (Article 10). A separate concession is granted to the holder of the permit for each exploitable deposit discovered during the period of the permit. Thus, under the Algerian oil legislation, the concessionaire's rights attach to an oil deposit rather than to an area and in consequence no relinquishment exists with respect to the concession. Subject to variations regarding the duration of the search permit and the extent of reduction of the permit area at each renewal, the oil legislation in Morocco and Tunisia with respect to relinquishment does not substantially differ from that applied in Algeria.

C. GOVERNMENT PARTICIPATION IN THE OIL INDUSTRY

Government participation in oil production is one of the key developments in the Middle East and North Africa. Many new concessions granted since 1957 have embodied an arrangement for Government participation in the enterprise. Considering the importance of this subject, a special chapter has been devoted to it in order to trace the development of the concept and discuss its present applications.

D. THE GRANT OF OFFSHORE CONCESSIONS IN TERRITORIAL WATERS AND THE CONTINENTAL SHELF

During the period under consideration oil technology was making progress with respect to the exploitation of oil resources in submarine areas. Such technological advance offered the possibility of oil exploitation underneath the waters of the Arabian Gulf. This led to two significant changes in the field of international law and practice: the extension of their territorial waters by the coastal States of the Arabian Gulf[16] and the assertion of their rights and jurisdiction over the continental shelf. These two developments constitute a vivid example of the interaction which occurs in some cases between industry, science and law.

In early times, no reference was made to the inclusion of territorial waters within the geographical area of oil concessions. The exploitation of oil in submarine areas was then unknown. The principal early concessions, such as D'Arcy's concession (1901), IPC's concession

---

[16] The Arabian Gulf and the Persian Gulf refer to the same sea inlet bordering upon the Arabian Peninsula, Kuwait, Iraq and Iran. Although the latter appellation was more frequent in Western literature, particularly at the time that Iran bore the name of Persia, present Arab usage favours the designation of the inlet as the Arabian Gulf or simply the Gulf.

from Iraq (1925) and AIOC's concession from Iran (1933) made no reference to territorial waters. However, territorial waters were included in Aramco's concession from Saudi Arabia (1933) and in KOC's concession from Kuwait (1934). Subsequent agreements made specific reference to territorial waters when the intention of the parties was to include them within the area of the concession.

As submarine oil exploitation became a reality, States realized the value of the mineral resources lying under their adjoining waters. This realization prompted an extension by the coastal States in the region of the Arabian Gulf of the width of their territorial waters. The traditional three-mile limit was abandoned by most Arab States and by Iran. On May 28, 1949, Saudi Arabia issued a Royal Decree fixing the width of the coastal sea at six nautical miles. Nine years later, this Royal Decree was repealed and replaced by a Royal Decree dated February 16, 1958 which extended the territorial sea to twelve nautical miles. The territorial sea adjacent to Kuwait was fixed at six miles by an Order of the Sheikh of Kuwait dated June 28, 1948. On April 12, 1959 Iran fixed the breadth of its territorial sea at twelve miles. It may be observed that five years earlier the agreement between the Consortium and Iran had fixed the maritime limit of the concession as being "a line lying three miles offshore from the lowest tide line of the mainland". Bahrain, Qatar and the Trucial Sheikhdoms did not extend their territorial waters but proclaimed their authority and jurisdiction over submarine areas adjacent to territorial waters.

The other development which was prompted by the possibility of submarine oil exploitation was the assertion by coastal States of their rights and jurisdiction over the continental shelf contiguous to territorial waters. The concept of the continental shelf was new and was first advanced in 1945 by the United States of America which set the precedent of claiming jurisdiction over mineral deposits in the continental shelf. This was followed by similar claims made by States around the Arabian Gulf. Saudi Arabia took the lead: by a Royal Proclamation of May 28, 1949, Saudi Arabia declared its ownership, jurisdiction and control over the subsoil and sea bed of those areas of the Persian Gulf[16a] seaward from the coastal sea that are contiguous to its coasts. In June 1949, Bahrain, Qatar, Kuwait and the Trucial Sheikhdoms issued proclamations making similar claims. In Novem-

---

[16a] See footnote 16.

ber 1957, Iraq asserted a similar claim on the continental shelf contiguous to Iraqi territorial waters.[17] Iran also asserted its claim to the
continental shelf. By a Law dated June 19, 1955, Iran declared that
the sea bed and subsoil adjacent to the Iranian coast are under
Iranian sovereignty. Four years later, by an Act promulgated on April
12, 1959 amending a previous Act of July 19, 1934 relating to the
breadth of the territorial sea and contiguous zone, Iran extended its
sovereignty over the territorial sea adjacent to its territory and over
its sea bed and subsoil to a distance of twelve miles. The Act further
provided that where Iranian coasts are adjacent or opposite to the
coast of another State, the boundary of the Iranian territorial sea
and that State is the median line.

These developments in the Arabian Gulf were part of a world-wide
movement intended to establish the rights of coastal States over the
mineral resources in contiguous submarine territories. These rights
received recognition by the Geneva Convention on the Continental
Shelf (1958). The Convention recognized that the coastal State exer-
cises over the continental shelf sovereign rights "for the purpose of
exploring it and exploiting its natural resources". The continental
shelf was defined as covering not only the sea bed and submarine
areas adjacent to the coast but also "outside the area of the territorial
sea, to a depth of 200 metres, or, beyond that limit, to where the depth
of the superjacent waters admits of the exploitation of the natural
resources of the said areas." Similar provisions were laid down with
respect to the sea bed and subsoil of submarine areas adjacent to
the coasts of islands. Regarding boundaries, the Convention provided
that, unless otherwise agreed or unless special circumstances require
a different solution, the boundary is the median line equidistant from
the baselines of the respective coasts.

Those principles have been translated into agreements which were
either concluded or are still in process of negotiation between some
of the coastal States in the Arabian Gulf. These agreements define
the boundaries of the sea bed outside territorial waters in the Arabian
Gulf between Saudi Arabia, Iran, Kuwait and Qatar. Oil fields, however, do not follow concession limits or international boundaries: it
is presumed, for example, that Aramco's Safaniya field and Arabian

---

[17] Lenczowski, *Oil and State in the Middle East,* pp. 126-129.

Oil Company's Khafji field belong to the same structure; the same situation exists with respect to two oil fields lying across the boundary of Iran and Iraq. Oil resources are sometimes shared between two countries without regard to sovereignty over the place of production. Thus, the agreement made between Saudi Arabia and Bahrain on February 22, 1958, fixed their marine and submarine boundaries, but in respect of one area therein defined (containing the Abu Sa'fah oil field), it was agreed that the exploitation of its oil resources will be carried out by Saudi Arabia on condition that one half of the net revenue accruing to Saudi Arabia from such exploitation shall belong to Bahrain. Similarly, the agreement concluded between Saudi Arabia and Kuwait on July 7, 1965 which divided the Neutral Zone between them has provided that this division shall be without prejudice to the rights of the parties to natural resources in the entirety of the divided zone, regardless as to whether such resources exist at present or may be discovered in the future.

The legal developments aforementioned coupled with the technological advance in submarine oil exploitation paved the way for the grant of offshore concessions within and without territorial waters. In 1948, Saudi Arabia confirmed Aramco's rights over the offshore area in the Arabian Gulf, including the sea bed and subsoil over which the Government has or may have dominion, control or ownership (Agreement of October 10, 1948). Since then, a number of offshore concessions were, and continue to be, granted in territorial waters and contiguous areas of the Arabian Gulf: the concession by the Ruler of Qatar to International Marine Oil Company, the concession by the Sheikh of Abu Dhabi to Abu Dhabi Marine Concessions Ltd., the concessions granted to Arabian Oil Company by Saudi Arabia and Kuwait off the territorial waters of the Neutral Zone, the concessions granted by Iran to AGIP and Pan American off the Iranian coast, the concession granted by Kuwait to Shell and the recent Iranian Offshore agreements made with five oil groups in January 1965.[18]

It may here be observed that the first submarine field to be discovered and exploited in the Middle East was the Safaniya field off

---

[18] By the end of 1965 twenty offshore concessions—all located outside territorial waters—had already been granted in the Arabian Gulf: see *Petroleum Press Service*, December 12, 1965, p. 461.

the shore of Saudi Arabia. This field was discovered by Aramco in 1951 and is believed to be the largest offshore oil field in existence.[19] Since then, a number of submarine fields (shown in Appendix II-B) were discovered in the Arabian Gulf. Some of the offshore concessions aforementioned are now producing oil. Their total production was estimated in May 1964 as approaching the one million barrel per day level. It has been remarked that the Arabian Gulf is the most promising and interesting scene of offshore activity in the world today.[20]

Offshore concessions were also granted by the U.A.R. in the Gulf of Suez and oil has been discovered there by the Compagnie Orientale des Pétroles d'Egypte (partly owned by the U.A.R. and partly by ENI) and more recently by Pan American.

It is of interest to note that the possibility of submarine oil exploitation has led to two disputes between the producing country and the concessionary company concerning the extent of concessionary rights over the subsoil underneath territorial waters and the continental shelf. Both disputes were resolved by arbitration.

The first dispute occurred between Petroleum Development (Qatar) Ltd. and the Ruler of Qatar in 1950 in the following circumstances. In a Proclamation dated June 8, 1949, the Ruler claimed jurisdiction over the continental shelf, i.e., the sea bed and subsoil beneath the high seas of the Arabian Gulf contiguous to the territorial waters of Qatar. On the basis of such Proclamation, the Ruler concluded an agreement with agents acting for International Marine Oil Company—a company then in process of formation—whereby he granted to the company oil concession rights over the sea bed and subsoil underlying waters in the Arabian Gulf which fell within his jurisdiction and lay beyond territorial waters contiguous to the mainland and islands of Qatar. Thereupon, Petroleum Development (Qatar) Ltd. which held concessionary rights "throughout the Principality of Qatar" under an agreement dated May 17, 1935, took objection to the grant of the new concession, claiming that it had a right under its concession to the sea bed and subsoil underneath the continental shelf. The Ruler disputed such contention as he also

---

[19] Standard Oil Company of California Bulletin, July 1958.

[20] *Petroleum Press Service,* May 1964, p. 187, which also gives a breakdown of offshore production in the Gulf.

disputed the right of Petroleum Development (Qatar) Ltd. to the sea bed and subsoil underneath territorial waters. The dispute was referred to arbitration and the arbitrator ruled that the concession included the sea bed and subsoil underneath territorial waters but did not extend to the sea bed and subsoil underneath the continental shelf. The award was not supported by any reasons.

Similar issues were involved in another dispute which occurred between Petroleum Development Ltd. and the Sheikh of Abu Dhabi about the same time. The dispute arose in circumstances similar to the previous one with the Ruler of Qatar. The company having objected to the grant of a concession to the sea bed and subsoil underneath the continental shelf to another company, a dispute arose as to whether Petroleum Development Ltd. had acquired rights to the sea bed and subsoil underneath territorial waters and the continental shelf. The concession originally made in favour of Petroleum Development Ltd. in 1939 as drawn in Arabic covered "the area of the lands which belong to the rule of the Ruler of Abu Dhabi and its dependencies and all the islands and the sea waters which belong to that area". The dispute was referred to arbitration. The award made by Lord Asquith of Bishopstone as umpire was delivered in 1951.[21] The umpire held that the claimants succeeded as to the subsoil of the territorial waters and that the Sheikh succeeded as to the subsoil of the continental shelf. In rejecting the argument made on behalf of the Sheikh that there was in 1939, i.e., the date of the grant of the concession, no word for "territorial waters" in the language of Abu Dhabi and that the Sheikh was quite unfamiliar with that conception, the umpire remarked that

> "Mr. Jourdain had none the less been talking 'prose' all his life because the fact was only brought to his notice somewhat late. Every State is owner and sovereign in respect of its territorial waters, their bed and subsoil, whether the Ruler has read the works of Bynkershoek or not. The extent of the Ruler's Dominion cannot depend on his accomplishments as an international jurist."

With the same learned knowledge and sense of humour, the umpire rejected the company's claim to the subsoil of the continental shelf and observed:

---

[21] *ICLQ* (1952), p. 247.

"I should certainly in 1939 have read the expression 'the sea waters which belong to that area' not only as including, but as *limited* to, the territorial belt and its subsoil. At that time neither contracting party had ever heard of the doctrine of the Continental Shelf, which as a legal doctrine did not then exist. No thought of it entered their heads. . . . Directed, as I apprehend I am, to apply a simple and broad jurisprudence to the construction of this contract, it seems to me that it would be a most artificial refinement to read back into the contract the implications of a doctrine not mooted till seven years later. . . ."

E. THE ENACTMENT OF PETROLEUM LEGISLATION

The march of progress extended to legislation. A number of countries enacted mining or petroleum laws regulating the exploitation of petroleum and the grant of oil concessions. The principal laws promulgated in this field are:

> The Tunisian Decree on Mines of 1948 as amended in 1953 and 1958;
> The Egyptian Laws of Mines and Quarries of 1953 and 1956;
> The Syrian Law of Mines and Quarries of 1954;[22]
> The Libyan Petroleum Law of 1955, amended in 1961, 1962 and 1965;[23]
> The Iranian Petroleum Act of 1957;
> The Petroleum Code of Morocco of 1958;
> The Sahara Petroleum Code of 1958;
> The Mining Law of Jordan of 1964.

In addition to the preceding legislation on petroleum and mining, one must also mention the Franco-Algerian Agreement on Hydrocarbons of 1965 which, though in terms an agreement between two States, regulates in the Protocol thereto annexed the activities relating to the production of petroleum under the Cooperative Association established by the two Governments in Algeria.

---

[22] In December 1964, a Legislative Decree was issued in Syria which prohibited the granting of any concession for the exploitation of mineral or petroleum resources as from the date of its coming into force: Legislative Decree No. 133 dated December 22, 1964, *Syrian Official Gazette* of December 31, 1964.

[23] The Libyan Petroleum Law of 1955 superseded the provisions of the Libyan Minerals Law of 1953 with respect to petroleum.

It may be observed that specific petroleum legislation, as distinct from general mining legislation, was enacted in five countries only: Libya, Iran, Morocco, Algeria and Tunisia. Reference will be made to relevant provisions of such legislation whenever pertinent to a matter under discussion. For this reason no attempt will be made here to describe the main features of such petroleum legislation.

The first comprehensive petroleum legislation was enacted in Libya in the form of the Petroleum Code of 1955. This Code superseded and replaced the provisions of the Libyan Minerals Law of 1953 with respect to petroleum. It was amended in 1961, 1962 and 1965 and several regulations were issued under it.

Iran followed suit by promulgating its Petroleum Act in 1957.

On July 21, 1958, Morocco issued a Dahir which embodied a Code for the search and exploitation of hydrocarbon deposits. The Code was supplemented by four decrees for its application.

On November 22, 1958, the Sahara Petroleum Code was promulgated. Some of its provisions were amended by the Evian Agreements concluded between Algeria and France in 1962. On July 29, 1965, an Agreement on Hydrocarbons was concluded between the Algerian and French Governments to which was annexed a Protocol establishing between them a Cooperative Association for the search and exploitation in common of hydrocarbons in Algeria. The Protocol governs and deals exhaustively with the relationships and activities arising under the Cooperative Association. The Sahara Petroleum Code, however, remains operative in certain respects, particularly in relation to some fiscal aspects as it continues to apply to companies that are outside the scope of the Cooperative Association.

In contrast to other Arab Governments possessing petroleum legislation, Tunisia did not promulgate a comprehensive petroleum code: its petroleum legislation is scattered among several legislative enactments. The first specific petroleum enactment was the Decree of December 13, 1948 which amended the Mining Decree of December 29, 1913 and established special provisions to encourage and facilitate the search for, and exploitation of, petroleum. Financially, the effect of this Decree was to limit the total amount of registration fees, taxes and royalty (not less than 10%) payable by an operator to 12½% of the total value of the crude oil produced. Apart from a number of other legislative enactments promulgated in 1953, the next important piece of legislation was the Law of March 23, 1958 which amended the Decree of 1948 by raising the royalty rate from 10 to 15% and by introducing an income tax of 50% on the oil operator's profits in Tunisia subject to subtraction of the royalty.

Since 1964 OPEC countries have been planning to unify petroleum legislation. In January of that year OPEC adopted a resolution which required its Secretary-General to invite experts to prepare a compilation of a code of uniform petroleum laws. A draft of a uniform oil law for Arab countries is currently under consideration by a Committee of the League of Arab States. The need for uniformity of petroleum legislation had already been stressed in 1958 by the Explanatory Statement accompanying the Sahara Petroleum Code. Although such Explanatory Statement was limited to the Sahara regions, yet the reasoning behind it applies, *mutatis mutandis,* to the Middle East in general. The Statement said:

> "It appears opportune to make the regime for petroleum operations uniform throughout the Sahara which constitutes an original and homogeneous geographical entity. . . . It would indeed be difficult to envisage that enterprises operating under the same technical, climatic and geographical conditions should be subject to different juridical and fiscal regimes which could be the source of artificial distortions of competition and could also be prejudicial to the common good."[24]

Although no uniform code of petroleum legislation has been enacted as yet in the OPEC countries, a substantial degree of harmony has been achieved in the financial conditions of oil concessions.

A number of countries have also enacted special tax legislation with respect to the profits of oil companies. Such tax legislation was promulgated in Saudi Arabia, Kuwait, Qatar, Bahrain, Algeria and Jordan. Its object in all cases was to impose a 50% income tax on the profits of oil companies and to regulate various matters incidental to the imposition of an income tax.

F. THE ESTABLISHMENT OF NATIONAL AND INTERNATIONAL AGENCIES CONCERNED WITH THE OIL INDUSTRY

Legislative developments were accompanied by the creation of national agencies and companies. Their nature and functions vary from one country to another.

---

[24] *Journal Officiel de la République Française* of November 23, 1958.

The National Iranian Oil Company (NIOC) was established in 1954. Apart from its own independent oil activities, which include exploration, production, marketing and the provision of "non-basic services" under the Consortium Agreement, NIOC has also entered, as we shall have occasion to see, into participation or partnership arrangements with a number of oil companies with respect to oil production in Iran.

In Libya, a Petroleum Commission was established under the Petroleum Law (1955) and vested with all powers in relation to the grant or revocation of concessions. However, this Commission was an administrative authority and not an organization designed to engage in the oil business. The Petroleum Commission was abolished in 1963 and its functions transferred to the Ministry of Petroleum Affairs.

In 1956, the U.A.R. established the General Petroleum Authority (GPA) which was reorganized in 1958 by Law No. 167. The GPA's main function was the general planning of petroleum policy with power to engage in, and supervise, all petroleum activities. In 1957, the U.A.R. set up the Egyptian General Petroleum Corporation (EGPC), the capital of which is owned by the Egyptian Government, through the Economic Institution, a State organization. In the agreements concluded by the U.A.R. with Phillips, Pan American and ENI, the EGPC is a joint grantee of the concessions.

In 1960, Kuwait established the Kuwait National Petroleum Corporation. This Corporation is state owned to the extent of 60% only, the balance of its capital belonging to Kuwaiti citizens. The Corporation is authorized to engage in the oil business.

In 1962, Saudi Arabia established the General Petroleum and Mineral Organization (Petromin) which has authority to engage, alone or in cooperation with others, in all kinds of mining activities.

Iraq formed the Iraqi National Oil Company by Law No. 11 of 1964. The objects of the Company were to operate in all phases of the oil industry, either itself, or through companies which it may form, or in cooperation with other companies or organizations.

In addition to the establishment of national companies, the oil exporting countries have also founded an international agency under the name of the Organization of Petroleum Exporting Countries, commonly called OPEC. This Organization was originally established by a resolution adopted on September 14, 1960 at a conference

of the principal oil exporting countries held at Baghdad. The conference was organized by Iraq and was attended by Iran, Kuwait,
Saudi Arabia and Venezuela. Three other oil exporting countries have
since joined the Organization, namely, Indonesia, Qatar and Libya.
The principal aims of OPEC were the unification of the oil policy
of Member States with a view to safeguarding their interests and, in
particular, the maintenance and the restoration to their previous level
of the prices of petroleum, the elimination of marketing expenses and
the expensing of royalties.[25]

In April 1965, OPEC approved a Statute containing the rules
relating to its objectives, membership and organization.

The Statute has defined the objectives of the Organization as
follows:

> "The principal aim of the Organization shall be the co-ordi-
> nation and unification of the petroleum prices of Member Coun-
> tries and the determination of the best means for safeguarding
> their interests, individually and collectively.
>
> "The Organization shall devise ways and means of ensuring
> the stabilization of prices of international crude oil markets with
> a view to eliminating harmful and unnecessary fluctuations.
>
> "Due regard shall be given at all times to the interests of the
> producing nations and to the necessity of securing a steady income
> to the producing countries; an efficient, economic and regular
> supply of petroleum to consuming nations; and a fair return on
> their capital to those investing in the petroleum industry."

The membership of the Organization is open to any country with
a substantial net export of crude petroleum which has fundamentally
similar interests to those of the Member Countries.

OPEC has three organs:

(1) The Conference which formulates general policy and
determines the appropriate ways for its implementation.

(2) The Board of Governors which directs the management
of the affairs of the Organization and implements the decisions
of the Conference.

---

[25] Agreement was reached between oil companies and most OPEC countries on the expensing of royalties and marketing expenses at the end of 1964.
The "expensing" of royalties means that, in computing the income tax payable by the oil concessionaire, royalty payments are treated as an expense instead of a credit against the income tax as had hitherto been the practice.

(3) The Secretariat which carries out the executive functions of the Organization.

In 1965, OPEC also established an Economic Commission as a permanent and specialized organ to assist it in promoting stability in international petroleum prices. The functions of the Economic Commission are to collect data and information, examine the position of petroleum prices on a permanent basis, study all relevant economic and other factors affecting petroleum prices and their structure and formulate and submit to the Conference appropriate recommendations.

(3) The Secretariat which carries out the executive functions of the Organisation.

In 1962 OPEC also established an Economic Commission as a permanent and specialized organ to assist it in promoting stability in international petroleum prices. The functions of the Economic Commission are to collect data and information, examine the position of petroleum prices on a permanent basis, study all relevant economic and other factors affecting petroleum prices and their structure and formulate and submit to the Conference appropriate recommendations.

Chapter II

Financial Conditions of Oil Concessions

The consideration offered by the concessionaire to the conceding State in return for the grant of the concession takes the form of one or more financial advantages.

These advantages are:

(1) Bonuses;

(2) Guaranteed expenditures on exploration;

(3) Rents;

(4) Royalties;

(5) Taxation, or equal sharing, of profits, including tax commutation payments;

(6) Ancillary benefits.

These advantages constitute the financial structure of oil concessions. We shall now examine the financial conditions in concession agreements, and, where applicable, in petroleum legislation.

SECTION 1. BONUSES

The making of bonus payments on the occasion of the grant of concessions was fairly common in the past. However, until 1948, bonuses or premiums on signature of oil agreements were almost all of a modest nature. The bonus paid on the occasion of the conclusion of the D'Arcy concession amounted to £.St. 20,000. Two agreements concluded in 1948 and 1949 with respect to the undivided interests of Saudi Arabia and Kuwait in the Neutral Zone raised the amount of bonuses. The agreement between Kuwait and Aminoil (1948) provided for the payment of a bonus of U.S. $7,250,000 (Article 3) while the agreement between Saudi Arabia and Pacific Western Oil

Corporation, subsequently Getty, provided for the payment upon signature of U.S. $9,500,000 (Article 4).

The practice of the payment of bonuses has now become widespread and their amount has increased as a result of the severe competition between applicants for the grant of concessions in promising areas. Naturally, no rule or principle exists with respect to the amount of bonuses which remain essentially a matter of agreement between the parties.

There exist different kinds of bonuses:

(1) bonuses payable on or following signature of the concession;

(2) bonuses payable on discovery of oil;

(3) bonuses payable on attaining certain levels of production.

The Iranian Petroleum Act (1957) envisaged the payment of cash bonuses upon the conclusion of oil agreements. Article 8 of the Act provided that in cases where the interest of NIOC in a "mixed organization" or a "joint structure"[1] is less than 50%, the person entering into any such relationship with NIOC for search, exploration or extraction operations shall pay to NIOC a lump sum as a cash bonus in addition to the rental provided under the Act. NIOC shall determine the amount of such cash bonus in accordance with the circumstances of the case. In practice, the payment of bonuses has extended to cases where NIOC has a 50% interest in the enterprise. The Act further provided that, apart from cases where NIOC acquires an interest in the "mixed organization" or "joint structure", persons making offers for the establishment of a "mixed organization" or a "joint structure" or an operating agreement with respect to search, exploration or extraction of oil shall specify the amount of the cash bonus which they are prepared to pay. The concession agreement granted to AGIP (1957) did not stipulate the payment of any cash bonus. The agreement made between NIOC and Pan American (1958) provided for the payment of a cash bonus of U.S. $30,000,000.

---

[1] The Iranian Petroleum Act (1957) has defined a "mixed organization" as "any juridical person which is owned in part by any person and in part by the National Iranian Oil Company" and has defined a "joint structure" as "any operating structure which is created jointly by the National Iranian Oil Company and one or more persons without a separate juridical personality resulting from such combination" (Article 1).

Iran's Offshore agreements (1965) have provided for payment of substantial cash bonuses following signature and for payment of production bonuses when production reaches a certain level.

In Libya, the Petroleum Law of 1955 did not provide for the payment of any cash bonuses. It is known, however, that concession agreements have embodied special benefits which are not published. Under the amending Decree-Law of 1961, applicants for concessions may include in their applications particulars of any economic and financial benefits which they are willing to offer in addition to the financial terms prescribed by the Petroleum Law. It is assumed that the economic and financial benefits to be offered include cash bonuses.

The bonus payments envisaged by the agreement concluded between Kuwait and Shell in 1961 are the highest known so far as having been undertaken to be paid by one company. The agreement provided for a signature bonus and for deferred bonuses, totalling £.St. 30,000,000. A signature bonus of £.St. 7,000,000 was paid on signature of the agreement. A deferred bonus of £.St. 7,000,000 is also payable on the fourth anniversary date or on the date upon which the net production of the company first reaches and maintains an average daily rate of 100,000 barrels over 30 consecutive days, whichever is earlier. Four further deferred bonuses of £.St. 4,000,000 each will become payable when net production of the company reaches certain levels of production, i.e., 200,000 barrels, 300,000 barrels, 400,000 barrels and 500,000 barrels.

The agreement between the Ruler of Ras Al Khaima and Kuamco Oil has envisaged a signature bonus of U.S. $400,000, a further bonus of U.S. $1,000,000 the payment of which is spread over four years, and a final bonus of U.S. $2,000,000 payable upon discovery of petroleum in commercial quantities.

The payment of bonuses on signature of the agreement, on the grant of the concession lease and on production reaching a certain level was also envisaged in Saudi Arabia's agreement with Auxirap (1965).

SECTION 2. GUARANTEED EXPENDITURES ON EXPLORATION

The assumption by the concessionaire of an obligation relating to a minimum and guaranteed expenditure on exploration during a

number of years is a new practice. First introduced by Turkey and
Libya, and later applied in Iran, it has now become a common condition of new concessions.

The early concession agreements granted to the concessionaire
the right to search for oil without imposing on him precise or burden-
some obligations in this respect, financial or otherwise. Moderate
expenditure requirements called "working obligations" were imposed
by Article 11 of the Libyan Petroleum Law of 1955. This Law
required the concession holder to commence exploratory operations
within 8 months and prescribed that the holder shall spend certain
minimum amounts per square kilometre each year. However, substantial obligations with respect to exploration expenditure were
imposed by Iran on the concessionaire in 1957 in the Petroleum Act
and agreements made thereunder. Article 9 of this Act provided that
NIOC may agree with a "mixed organization" or a "joint structure"
that instead of payment of rent, the other party will assume the obligation of meeting all or part of the expenses of exploration up to the
discovery of petroleum in commercially exportable quantities. NIOC
was required to fix the minimum amount of such expenditure having
due regard to the circumstances of each case. If on the termination
of exploration operations there is an unspent surplus, NIOC will have
the option to demand payment of half of the surplus for the account
of the Iranian Government or to require the other party to spend
the whole of the surplus on future operations of search, exploration
or extraction. Obligations with respect to exploration expenditures
have been imposed in substantial amounts in all oil agreements made
under the Iranian Petroleum Act. These agreements will be examined in greater detail in Chapter IV while discussing participation
by Government in the oil industry.

Thus Iran generalized two practices with respect to exploration
expenditures:

(1) The imposition of substantial minimum amounts to be
expended by NIOC's partner on exploration;

(2) The assumption by NIOC's partner of the burden of
exploration expenditure until the date of discovery of oil.

The precedent set by Iran in this respect was followed in the
U.A.R. and an exploration expenditure obligation is found in oil

concessions granted by this country. These concessions will be considered in greater detail in Chapter IV.

The agreement made between Hadramaut and Pan American Hadramaut Oil Company (1961) also made provision for the expenditure of certain minimum amounts on exploration operations.

Certain concessions spell out the concessionaire's obligation with reference to exploration in terms of aggregate drilling depth instead of in the form of monetary expenditure. Such provisions will be reviewed in discussing drilling and exploration obligations in Section 6 of Chapter III.

SECTION 3. RENTS

Most concessions make provision for the payment of rent, though concessions exist under which no rent is payable, such as the Iran-AGIP agreement (1957) and the Jordan-Mecom concession (1964). Some early agreements provided for certain fixed payments though not specifically described as rent. There exists no uniformity among oil concessions with respect to the payment of rent and variations even occur in the rental provisions of concessions granted by the same country.

Rental payments vary in their logic and in their amounts. In some concessions, rents decrease or even cease upon commencement of production and payment of royalties, as in Kuwait, while in others rents increase with the life of the concession, as in Iran.

Rents take the form of fixed amounts or are related to acreage.

A recent development in relation to rents was evolved as a consequence of joint venture agreements made between some Governments and oil companies. These agreements generally provide for an undertaking by the Government's partner to expend certain amounts on exploration in lieu of rent. However, rent becomes payable either after the exploration period, as in Iran, or upon exploitation, as in the U.A.R.

We shall now review the rental provisions in some recent concessions.

Under the agreement made in 1952 between Shell Exploration Company and the Ruler of Qatar, the company agreed to pay an annual rent at the rate of £.St. 75,415 up to the date of commencement of regular exports of oil, such rent to be reduced thereafter to

£.St. 37,707 per annum until termination of the concession.

The amounts of rents payable under the Libyan Petroleum Law of 1955 vary with the zone in which the concession is located and with the life of the concession, such rents rising upon the finding of petroleum in commercial quantities (Article 13). The amounts fixed for such rents were revised upwards in 1961.

The two offshore agreements made with the Arabian Oil Company provided for payment of rentals as follows: the agreement made in 1957 between Saudi Arabia and Japan Petroleum Trading Company, subsequently assigned to Arabian Oil Company, stipulated the payment of U.S. $1,500,000 as annual rent, while the agreement made between Kuwait and Arabian Oil Company (1958) provided for the payment of an annual rent of U.S. $1,500,000 until oil is discovered in commercial quantities.

The Iranian Petroleum Act provided in Article 9 that every person who enters into an agreement with NIOC shall pay an annual rent to be determined by NIOC and which is compatible with the extent of the area and the characteristics of the zone envisaged for exploration and extraction and, in particular, with the possibilities of discovery of petroleum and the facility of marketing. Iran's agreements with Pan American and Sapphire stipulated the payment of rent as from the 13th year of the agreement and during subsequent years at the rate of $400 per square kilometre, rising to $480 and eventually to $600 per square kilometre. During the first twelve years, the operator is subject to exploration expenditure but not to any rental obligation. Iran's recent Offshore agreements (1965) stipulated the payment of rent as from the date of commercial production at the rate of $400 per annum per square kilometre, rising progressively to $1,050 per square kilometre.

The U.A.R.'s practice with respect to rentals has varied from that followed in Iran. In the U.A.R.'s agreements with Phillips and Pan American, a distinction was made between the period of exploration and the period of exploitation. During the period of exploration the concessionaire undertakes to expend certain minimum amounts on exploration in lieu of paying rent. However, upon exploitation, rent becomes due at the rate of £.Eg. 25,000 per annum for each exploration block converted into a development lease.

The agreement between Kuwait and Shell (1961) provided for

the payment of rent at the rate of £.St. 1,000,000 per annum until the date of discovery of crude petroleum in commercial quantities, or until the second anniversary date, whichever shall be the earlier, and thereafter at the rate of £.St. 2,000,000 per annum until the date of export of crude petroleum.

The agreement between Hadramaut and Pan American (1961) provided for the payment of annual rentals throughout the years of the concession.

Rental payments rising progressively every five years and ranging from $50 to $500 for each square kilometre were stipulated in Saudi Arabia's agreement with Auxirap (1965).

The conclusion to be reached from this review is that no uniform rule exists regarding the rent payable under oil concessions as the rent varies with time, country and concession.

SECTION 4. ROYALTIES

We have already observed that in the past royalties constituted the principal financial feature of oil concessions. Though royalties have continued until the present day to be a standard term of concessions, they have ceased to represent the main consideration derived by the producing country.

We shall now examine various aspects relating to royalties.

A. Kinds and Rates of Royalties

Four kinds of royalties have existed in the Middle East:

(1) Fixed cash royalties related to tonnage of the crude oil produced. The standard rate in the past was either four shillings gold or in some countries three rupees per ton of net crude oil produced and saved after deduction of water, foreign substances and oil required for company operations. The rate of four shillings gold first appeared in Iraq's conventions with IPC (1925)[2] and the Khanaqin Oil Company (1926) and subsequently in the agreements made by AIOC (1933) and Aramco (1933). A uniform rate of three rupees per ton was stipulated in the concessions granted to KOC in Kuwait (1934); to Anglo-Persian Oil Company in Qatar (1935); to Petroleum Concessions Ltd. in

---

[2] Article 10.

the Sultanate of Muscat and Oman (1937) and to Abu Dhabi Petroleum Company (1939). A royalty rate of Rs. 3.8.0 was stipulated in Bapco's concession (1934).

Towards mid-century the rate of royalties was substantially increased in two concessions granted with respect to the Neutral Zone: Kuwait's concession to Aminoil (1948) stipulated a royalty of U.S. $2.50 per ton (Article 3) while Saudi Arabia's concession to Getty (1949) stipulated a royalty of U.S. $0.55 per barrel (Article 5).[3]

However, in most, though not all, cases such fixed cash royalties were abandoned, as we shall soon see, in favour of a royalty expressed as a percentage of the export price of crude oil.

(2) Cash royalties related to both tonnage and company dividends. The only instance of such a composite payment was found in AIOC's concession (1933). Article 10 of this concession provided that the company shall pay:

(i) an annual royalty of four shillings per ton of petroleum sold or exported; and

(ii) a sum equal to 20% of the distribution to the ordinary stockholders of the company in excess of the sum of £.St. 671,250, whether the distribution was made as dividends or carried to the reserves of the company.

(3) Variable cash royalties increasing or decreasing with the company's profits. This was the pattern found in the concessions granted by Iraq to the IPC group of companies. Under those agreements, the concessionaire undertook to pay to the Government a royalty per ton of oil won and saved, subject to the usual deductions, at the rate of four shillings gold for the period of 20 years after completion of a pipeline to a port for export. Following such period of 20 years, the rate of royalty was to be increased or reduced for each period of 10 years in accordance with a formula based upon the percentage of increased or decreased profit or loss—profit being defined as the difference between the average market price per ton and the average cost per ton of producing, transporting, refining and distributing.

---

[3] The equivalence between barrels and tons of crude oil depends upon its specific gravity and varies from 6.6 to 8 barrels approximately per metric ton.

(4) Royalties in the form of a percentage of net oil production or its cash equivalent based upon posted or, in a few cases, realized prices. This is the modern and fairly generalized form of royalty today.

The practice of the payment to the producing country of a royalty in kind or in cash at Government's option appears to have been introduced in the Middle East by the agreements made between Iraq and the IPC group of companies. The earliest provision in any effective oil concession providing for the right of the producing country to take a percentage of crude oil produced by the concessionaire or its equivalent in cash is found in the concession granted by Iraq on April 20, 1932 to British Oil Development Company (B.O.D.) whose interests were subsequently acquired by the Mosul Petroleum Company, an IPC subsidiary. The same provision was included in the concession granted by Iraq to the Basrah Petroleum Company on July 29, 1938. These two concessions recognized the Government's right:

(i) to a royalty of four shillings gold per ton of crude oil won and saved (less certain agreed deductions) and, in addition,

(ii) to receive free of cost at well-head 20% of all petroleum won and saved by the company. In respect of such 20% no royalty shall be payable. The Government could take such 20% in kind and any part not so taken in kind shall be sold by the Government to the company and purchased by the company, in the case of B.O.D.'s concession (Article 12), at prices to be ascertained on a basis to be agreed upon; and at a fair free market price prevailing at well-head in Rumania or, failing such a free market price in Rumania, at a price to be determined by arbitration in the case of the Basrah Petroleum Company (Article 14). In both cases, it was agreed that the Government shall not export or sell for export in crude or refined form any part of the petroleum taken in kind.

On February 3, 1952 Iraq and the IPC group of companies reached a new agreement that revised the financial terms of their three concessions on the basis of the equal sharing concept. At the same time, the original royalty provisions of four shillings gold per ton—plus a 20% share of crude oil produced as envisaged in the conventions of the Basrah Petroleum Company and the Mosul Petroleum Company—were abandoned in favour of a new system of royalty introduced for the first time in the Middle East. Articles 3 and 10 of the new agreement gave to the Government the right to take in kind up to $12\frac{1}{2}$% of the net production of the companies or a sum equal to the value at posted prices of oil not taken in kind. A royalty rate of $\frac{1}{8}$ has been current for a long time in the United States of America.

This provision now represents the standard, though not uniform, rate of royalty and has received application in oil concessions in Kuwait, Libya, Iran, Algeria and the Sheikhdoms in the Arabian Gulf. Although the standard rate of royalty is normally $12\frac{1}{2}$% of net production, such rate is not invariable and recent concessions have deviated therefrom. Royalty rates today range generally between $12\frac{1}{2}$% and 20%.

We shall now review the royalty provisions in force today under the principal oil concessions in the Middle East and North Africa.

The royalty in the Qatar-Shell Overseas agreement (1952) was fixed at 4 shillings 6 pence for each ton of exported oil.

In the Consortium's agreement with Iran (1954), the term royalty is not used but the equivalent payment is described as a "stated payment". The Consortium's agreement provided for a "stated payment" at the rate of $12\frac{1}{2}$% of the applicable posted price of crude oil (Article 22). NIOC has, however, the right to elect to take crude oil in lieu of all or part of the "stated payment" (Article 23).

The Iranian Petroleum Act of 1957 stated that in cases where the interest of NIOC in a "mixed organization" or a "joint structure" is less than 50%, or where an agreement is concluded with any person to operate independently of a "mixed organization" or a "joint structure", the operator must bind himself to supply in kind to NIOC, if the latter so requests, one-eighth of the total production, the value of which, calculated at posted prices, shall be deductible from his tax liability.

The agreement made between NIOC and AGIP (1957) made provision for the payment of a royalty of $12\frac{1}{2}$% of the posted price but the two agreements made with Pan American and Sapphire in 1958 did not envisage any royalties or "stated payments". Iran's Offshore agreements of 1965 specifically state that the parties shall not be required to make any "stated payments". The absence of any royalty or "stated payment" in the recent Iranian Offshore agreements may be explained, however, by the fact that NIOC's partner assumes a minimum income tax liability in an amount equal to $12\frac{1}{2}\%$ of the value at posted prices of such partner's share in the crude oil produced.

Under the agreement made between Kuwait and KOC in 1955, royalty on crude oil was fixed at 11 shillings sterling per ton. The new royalty was stated to be approximately $12\frac{1}{2}\%$ of the then existing posted prices. It was further provided that the royalty will be variable so as to keep it at approximately this percentage.

The Libyan Petroleum Law, as amended, provided that the concession holder shall pay a royalty of $12\frac{1}{2}\%$ of the posted price. The Law further provided that the royalty shall be abated by surface rents of certain amounts. The royalty was payable in cash only but the Law as amended in 1961 gave the Government the option to receive the royalty either in cash or in kind.

The agreement between Saudi Arabia and Japan Petroleum Trading Company (1957), subsequently Arabian Oil Company, introduced in Article 14 a new rate of royalty equal to 20% of the crude oil produced. Government is entitled at its election to take such royalty either in cash or in kind. If the Government elects to receive the royalty in cash, the sum is calculated on the basis of value at posted prices. It may incidentally be remarked here that Saudi Arabia receives at present three different rates of royalties:

(1) The equivalent of four shillings gold per ton from Aramco,[4] plus five cents (U.S. $0.05) per barrel for offshore production;

(2) Fifty-five U.S. cents per barrel from Getty; and

(3) Twenty percent of the value of crude oil at posted prices from Arabian Oil Company.

The agreement made between Kuwait and the Arabian Oil Com-

---

[4] Aramco's original concession of 1933 stipulated a royalty of four shillings gold or its equivalent per ton of net crude oil but made no provision for an option in favour of the Government to take the royalty in kind. The agreement made on January 25, 1965 between the parties on the expensing of royalties granted an option to the Government to take crude oil in lieu of royalty, if desired.

pany with respect to Kuwait's interest in the offshore of the Neutral
Zone has provided for a similar royalty of 20%.

The royalty rate in Algeria is 12½% in accordance with the Sahara Petroleum Code of 1958 (Article 63).

Under the Decree of December 13, 1948, the royalty rate in
Tunisia was fixed at 10%. However, such rate was subsequently increased to 15%. The concessions granted to Conorada (1958) and
Societa Olli Minerali (1959) have provided for a royalty at the rate
of 15%.

The U.A.R. oil concessions have provided for a higher rate of
royalty than 12½%. The two agreements made with Phillips and
Pan American in 1963 stated that the Government shall be entitled
to a royalty of 15% which Government may elect to take in cash or
in kind. In its agreement with ENI (1963), the royalty was fixed at
20% of the total quantity of petroleum produced from an exploitation block or blocks up to an aggregate area not exceeding 50% of
the original area of the exploration block or blocks. For the remaining 50% of the said exploration block which may be converted into
part of an exploitation block or one or more exploitation blocks, the
royalty levied by the Government on the total quantity of petroleum
produced therefrom was fixed at 30%.

These agreements—except that made with ENI—further contained a provision enabling the amendment of the rate of royalty
under certain conditions. They provided that, for the purpose of fur-
thering or prolonging the economic development of certain development leases, the Government may reduce the royalty if it is satisfied
that the cost of production, including the amount paid for taxes,
prohibits the undertaking of profitable development of the production, or if the cost of production has increased to a point which does
not permit of profitable development. The royalty so reduced may be
increased by Government up to the original level when it considers
that the reasons for making the reduction have ceased.

The U.A.R.'s agreement with Pan American made in 1964 stipulated a royalty of 20%. However, this agreement contained a new
provision which stated that the royalty shall be reduced to 15%
when:

> (1) Pan American has fully amortized its exploration obli-
> gations mentioned in the agreement;

(2) Fifty percent of the company's taxable profits exceed 20% of its gross income.

The Kuwait-Shell agreement (1961) provided for the payment of a royalty of 5 shillings per ton of net production prior to the commencement of regular exports and for a royalty equal to 12½% of the posted price for every barrel of net production after the date of commencement of regular exports.

The agreement between Hadramaut and Pan American (1961) stipulated a royalty equal to 12½% with Government's election to take such royalty in cash or in kind.

The agreement made between the Ruler of Ras Al Khaima and Kuamco Oil envisaged a royalty equivalent to 12½% of posted prices.

Jordan's agreement with Mecom (1964) provided for a royalty of 16⅔% of the posted price payable in cash.

Saudi Arabia's agreement with Auxirap (1965) provided for the payment of a graduated royalty, in kind or in cash at Government's option, at a rate of 20% of the crude oil produced, subject to reduction to 15% if the annual production does not exceed an average of 60,000 barrels per day and to 17% if such production exceeds 60,000 but does not exceed 80,000 barrels per day. If the Government elects to take the royalty in kind, the oil will be delivered FOB at the concessionaire's seaboard terminal. If the Government elects to receive the royalty in cash, the sum due is equal to the value of the oil it represents at posted price.

Before concluding this discussion on the various kinds of royalties in existence today in the Middle East and North Africa, it may be remarked that a type of royalty graduated to production appears to be developing in some countries. We have seen instances of royalties, the rate of which may be decreased in relation to production costs or to levels of production in the case of certain concessions granted by Egypt and Saudi Arabia. The Petroleum Code of Morocco of July 21, 1958, lays down a progressive royalty graduated to the volume of production commencing with a rate of 6% if production exceeds 50,000 tons and reaching a rate of 14% at a level of production in excess of one million tons per annum, though in no case is the total royalty to exceed a rate of 12½%.

B. CALCULATION OF ROYALTIES.

The rule prevailing in most concessions is for calculation of the royalty on the basis of posted prices. This rule, however, does not apply in all cases, and there are various instances in which royalties are not related to posted prices. Such variations from the general rule are encountered, for instance, in Libya, before the amendment of the Law in 1961, Algeria, and the U.A.R. The calculation in those countries has been based upon "realized", as distinct from posted, prices.

The Libyan Petroleum Law had originally envisaged that the royalty rate was to be calculated on well-head value which was defined as the "average free competitive market price" FOB Libyan seaboard terminal with adjustments for quality and gravity minus transportation and handling costs. However, under an amendment enacted in 1961, it was provided that the royalty shall be calculated on the basis of the "prevailing price", meaning the price FOB seaboard terminal for Libyan crude oil of the gravity and quality concerned, arrived at by reference to free market prices. The amendment made on November 20, 1965 has prescribed that the $12\frac{1}{2}\%$ royalty shall be calculated on the basis of applicable posted prices. This amendment was reflected in modifications agreed to by the Libyan Government and the various concessionaires on January 20, 1966.

The Sahara Petroleum Code of 1958 stated in Article 63 that the method of calculating the value of the royalty will be defined by the concession convention or by the model convention to be prepared under the Code.[5] The model convention, approved in 1961, provided that the royalty shall be based upon field prices determined at the end of each calendar quarter on the basis of average commercial prices resulting from export agreements or from sales to refining and marketing companies taking into account freight rates (Article C38).

The U.A.R. also adopts realized prices as the basis for the calculation of royalties. Its agreement with Phillips (1963) provided that royalty, whether taken in kind or in cash, shall be calculated on the basis of the weighted average export price received for crude oil by

---

[5] *Journal Officiel de la République Française* of January 8, 1961, p. 340. This model convention was replaced by another convention approved by Decree dated September 16, 1961: *Journal Officiel de la République Française* of September 17, 1961.

EGPC or Phillips from non-affiliated purchasers during the period for which the said royalty is due, such price to be computed back to the field main storage tank. If it is not feasible so to determine the price, it shall be assessed by agreement between the parties. The subsequent two agreements made with Pan American in 1963 and 1964 have provided for a similar computation of the value of the royalty.

In accordance with a recent resolution adopted by OPEC in April 1966, it was recommended that no petroleum rights be granted or contracts be made by member countries unless royalty payments (and income tax liabilities) are calculated on the basis of posted or reference prices.

C. THE EXPENSING OF ROYALTIES.

The expensing of royalties is a question which engaged the attention of OPEC and the producing countries for over two years. In its inception, the equal profit sharing concept was implemented upon the understanding that the total of the royalty and the income tax paid by the concessionaire will be equal to 50% of net profits and will represent the producing country's overall share. Consequently, royalty payments were not deducted from income as an expense item in computing the income tax, but were instead credited against the tax payable to the producing country. In 1962, OPEC challenged this approach. It was argued that the royalty is a payment which is ordinarily made to the owner of the ground in consideration of the depletion of the natural resource and for that reason should be paid to the Government independently of the tax. After prolonged negotiations that lasted until the end of 1964, agreement was reached between the oil companies and most of the Governments concerned on what is described in the oil industry's language as the "expensing" of royalties. The principle underlying the agreement is henceforth to treat royalty payments as an expense in computing income tax instead of a credit against the income tax.

D. MINIMUM ROYALTIES.

Several concessions have embodied provisions for the payment of minimum royalties. IPC's agreement with Iraq (1931) which amended the original concession made provision for a guaranteed minimum royalty of £.St. 400,000 per annum for a period of 20 years. Aminoil's agreement with Kuwait (1948) stipulated a minimum royalty of $625,000 per annum. Getty's concession (1949) laid down an annual minimum royalty of $1,000,000. Aramco's Offshore concession (1948) guaranteed to the Government an annual minimum royalty from offshore oil of $2,000,000. The agreement between Saudi Arabia and Japan Petroleum Trading Company (1957) envisaged an annual minimum royalty of $2,500,000. A similar minimum royalty was stipulated in Kuwait's agreement with Arabian Oil Company. Saudi Arabia's concession to Auxirap (1965) contained a provision for an annual minimum royalty of $1,500,000.

The object of a minimum royalty is to ensure a fixed financial consideration in favour of the producing country regardless of production, its volume or value. A royalty based on units of production or values also provides a minimum dependent, however, on production. In the usual applications of the 50-50 principle prior to 1965 the royalty was credited against the tax and was treated as a part of the Government's 50% share. When, however, the royalty and other payments that were taken into consideration as credits exceeded 50% of the profits, the royalty was generally not reduced.[6] Since 1965 the royalty has in most cases been considered a payment in addition to the tax.

The recent agreements on the expensing of royalties had the effect of untying, so to speak, the royalty from the tax and making it payable independently of the amount of the tax, subject to its being taken as a deduction from income. The fiscal effect, therefore, of the expensing of royalties is not limited to the conversion of the royalty from a tax credit into an expense item but has resulted also in the conversion of the royalty in all cases into a minimum payment due and payable by the concessionaire regardless of the existence of profits or of any income tax liability.

---

[6] In Libya and Algeria, however, the rule was otherwise. Under Article 14 (b) of the Libyan Petroleum Law before its amendment in 1961 and 1965, if the total payments, including royalty, for any year exceeded 50% of the profits, the concessionaire was entitled to deduct the excess. Similarly, under Article 65 of the Sahara Petroleum Code, if the royalty (*redevance*) for any year exceeded the taxable profit, one half of the difference could be deducted from the tax.

SECTION 5. TAXATION AND EQUAL PROFIT SHARING

In this Section we will examine the main aspects of the income tax arrangements introduced since mid-century in order to implement the equal sharing concept. It was a natural consequence of the implementation of the profit sharing concept to create an interest, previously inexistent, on the part of the producing countries in various factors which affect their share in the profits, such as the prices of crude oil, deductible expenses, amortization, discounts and the volume of production. We shall limit ourselves, however, to the fiscal and legal aspects involved, namely, the rate of tax, the taxable income, deductible expenses, tax subtractions, tax commutation payments and tax limitations. Reference will also be made to agreements which have deviated from the equal profit sharing concept or from the principle of the territoriality of taxes.

A. TAXATION OF PROFITS AT THE RATE OF 50%

For almost fifty years, the general practice in the Middle East had been to stipulate a complete immunity of the oil concessionaire from taxation of every kind, present or future. Such immunity was either absolute or was granted in consideration of tax commutation payments. Contractual provisions in oil concessions relating to tax commutation payments will be mentioned in subsection F. There was one exception to this general practice of tax immunity: the concession granted by Iraq to IPC in 1925. Article 27 of this concession provided that no other, or higher, taxes, impositions, duties, fees or charges shall be imposed upon the company or upon its property or employees within Iraq than those ordinarily imposed from time to time upon other industrial undertakings or upon their property or employees. However, this provision was superseded by an exchange of letters dated March 24, 1931 which exempted the company from all taxation of whatever nature in consideration of certain annual payments therein defined.

Some of the earlier concessions, particularly those made with the Sheikhs of the Arabian Gulf, were even silent upon the question of exemption from taxation, the reason being that taxes in those areas were virtually unknown.

Apart from IPC's convention of 1925, the only other concession during the first half of the century that departed from the usual pattern of either exemption or commutation of taxation was Getty's concession in the Neutral Zone (1949). Article 49 of the agreement first laid down the principle of freedom from taxation for the company, its property and all of its activities in connection with the development and exploitation of the concession, but then went on to provide that taxes may be levied by the Government against the company on account of its operations, if and only to the extent that a credit of the full amount of such taxes is allowed against the amount of any tax otherwise payable by the company to any other government.

At mid-century a radical change occurred. The concept of the equal sharing of oil profits was introduced in the relationships between oil companies and producing countries and was implemented in different ways which varied in accordance with concessions or legislations. The equal sharing concept was implemented either in the form of the submission by the concessionaire to an income tax at the rate of 50%, or of an undertaking to make a total sum of payments which, including existing taxes or a surtax or a make-up payment, amounted to 50% of profits, or in the form of an agreement providing for a straight division of net profits.

The first legislation taxing the profits of oil companies was enacted in Saudi Arabia in accordance with a Royal Decree dated December 27, 1950. This Royal Decree instituted an income tax on companies engaged in the production of petroleum or other hydrocarbons resulting in combined payments of royalty and tax amounting to 50% of their "net operating income," the latter expression being defined to mean net income before deduction of royalties and income taxes. On December 30, 1950 Aramco submitted to the income tax imposed by the said Royal Decree. Article 1 of the agreement concluded between Aramco and the Government of Saudi Arabia provided that in no case shall the total of income taxes and all other taxes, royalties, rentals and exactions of the Government for any year exceed 50% of the company's gross income after such gross income has been reduced by Aramco's costs of operation, including loss and depreciation, but not reduced by taxes, royalties, rentals or exactions.

Kuwait was the first to follow the example set in Saudi Arabia. By Decree dated December 29, 1951, the Ruler of Kuwait instituted an income tax equal to 50% of the income of corporations engaged in the production, purchase and sale of petroleum after deduction from such income of costs and depreciation. By an agreement dated December 30, 1951, KOC admitted the applicability to it and its owner companies of the income tax imposed by the said Decree. A new and more general Income Tax Decree was issued in 1955 in substitution for the Income Tax Decree of 1951, but such Decree did not affect the income tax rate.

By an agreement made in 1952 between the Ruler of Qatar and Shell Overseas Exploration Company, it was agreed that the Ruler will receive 50% of the "Oil Profit", as defined, made up of income tax and convention payments. Rent, payment for security and taxes were excluded from the definition of convention payments. If the total of income tax and convention payments was less than an amount equal to 50% of the "Oil Profit", the company undertook to pay a sum equal to the deficiency, such payment being described as a make-up payment. "Oil Profit" was defined as the profit arising in Qatar on exported oil and other substances produced by the company in the concession area and exported from Qatar.

The same development occurred in Bahrain in December 1952. On December 6, 1952 the Ruler issued a Decree imposing a 50% tax on the income derived from sales of petroleum and other natural hydrocarbons produced and extracted in Bahrain. On December 16, 1952 Bapco submitted to this Tax Decree. The said Tax Decree was superseded and replaced by the Bahrain Income Tax Regulation of 1955 imposing the same rate of tax. The company submitted to this new Decree on November 29, 1955.

The Iran-Consortium agreement (1954) also provided for payment by Trading Companies[7] and Operating Companies of Iranian

---

[7] Trading Companies are subsidiary companies formed by the Consortium members to carry out their trading operations. Article 18 of the Iran-Consortium agreement states that any Consortium member may assign to one or more subsidiaries nominated by it to act as a Trading Company or Trading Companies a part or all of that Consortium member's rights and obligations pertaining to the purchase and resale of crude oil, provided that no such assignment shall relieve such Consortium member of its obligations under the agreement. Any Trading Company to which such an assignment is made shall be deemed to become a party to the agreement. Trading Companies shall purchase from NIOC all crude oil produced by the Exploration and Producing Company other than crude oil required for company operations or internal

income tax. In accordance with the Iranian Income Tax Act of 1949, the rate of tax on companies had been fixed at 50% of their net income.

The Libyan Petroleum Law of 1955, as amended in 1961, provided in Article 14 that the concession holder shall pay such income tax and other taxes and imposts as are payable under the laws of Libya but shall not be subject to any form of taxation or other exaction of such nature as to render him liable to taxation or to other duties not payable by other persons in general operating in Libya other than fees, royalties and surface rents made payable under the Petroleum Law. It was provided, however, that

> (1) If in respect of any year the total amount of the fees, rents, royalties[8] payable under the Petroleum Law, income taxes and other taxes for which a concession holder is liable in respect of his operations falls short of 50% of his profits, the concession holder shall pay such sum by way of surtax as will make the total payments equal to 50% of his profits;

> (2) If in respect of any year the total amount of the fees, rents, royalties payable under the Petroleum Law, income taxes and other taxes for which the concession holder is liable exceeds 50% of his profits, he shall be entitled to deduct from his tax payments a sum equal to such excess.[9]

Ordinarily, the profit sharing arrangements were introduced without waiting for recoupment by the concessionaire of exploration and development expenditures. Such expenditures would be amortized in the ordinary course of business. In one case, however, the implementation of the equal profit sharing concept was conditioned upon the recovery by the concessionaire of all costs incurred for survey, ex-

---

consumption and may also purchase from NIOC any natural gas produced. Trading Companies are also envisaged under the Iranian Offshore agreements of 1965. Article 30 (9) of each of such agreements defines a Trading Company as any company wherever incorporated, duly registered in Iran, which derives income from selling in Iran crude oil produced under this agreement which it has purchased from the parties to the agreement.

[8] Under the amending Law of November 20, 1965 the royalty amounting to 12½% of the value of exported crude oil is excepted from the operation of this provision (Article II).

[9] Before the amendment of the Law, the concession holder was entitled to deduct the excess "from his total payments".

ploration and development. The concession granted by the Sultan of Muscat and Oman on January 17, 1953 to Philpryor Corporation, subsequently assigned to Cities Service Company, envisaged the payment of a royalty of $12\frac{1}{2}\%$ in cash or in kind of the oil produced until such time as all costs incurred by the company in its survey, exploration and development of oil are recovered, but thereafter, in lieu of the royalty of $12\frac{1}{2}\%$ or its monetary equivalent, the concession provides that "the royalty to be paid to the Sultan shall be equivalent to the amount which would have been payable if the pertinent provisions of the present agreement between the Government of Saudi Arabia and Aramco had been incorporated into this concession. In essence, this involves payment to the Sultan of 50% of the net profits accruing to the company from its operations hereunder . . .".

The Sahara Petroleum Code (1958) stated in Article 62 that the holders of mining titles are subject to the royalty (*redevance*) at the rate of $12\frac{1}{2}\%$ and to a direct tax on profits. The direct tax on profits is determined as follows:

(1) If the amount of taxable profits for any year exceeds the amount of the royalty, the difference between such two amounts is subject to a direct tax of 50%.

(2) If the amount of the royalty for any year exceeds the amount of taxable profits, a sum equal to one half of the difference between such two amounts may be deducted from other or future direct taxes due by the taxpayer (Article 65).

The income tax rate imposed by the Sahara Petroleum Code is not applicable to the companies and activities envisaged by the Franco-Algerian Agreement on Hydrocarbons (1965). The fiscal provisions of this Agreement will be considered in subsection H, *post*.

The Petroleum Code of Morocco (1958) provided that if the total sums paid by the concessionaire as "surface" taxes, royalty and duties are less than 50% of the profits, the concessionaire will pay a surtax equal to the difference between such total sums and one half of the profits (Article 31).

The Kuwait-Shell agreement (1961) provided that the Emir shall receive the greater of 50% of the "Oil Profit" (ascertained on the basis of posted prices) or 57% of the "Oil Income" (ascertained on the basis of realizations).

A 50% tax was also stipulated in the agreements concluded between the U.A.R. and Phillips in 1963 and between the U.A.R. and Pan American in 1963 and 1964. These agreements stated that the Government shall receive in any tax year by way of royalty, rental and taxes 50% of the net profits realized by the concessionaires as a result of their activities conducted in the U.A.R. under the agreements, provided that the amount the Government shall receive shall not in any tax year be less than the value of the royalty. In the event that the total amount of rentals, royalties, income taxes and other taxes, duties and imposts is less than 50% of the concessionaires' net profits for any tax year, the concessionaires shall pay to the Government an additional sum by way of an additional tax on income sufficient to make the total of payments to Government equal to 50% of net profits. However, these agreements guaranteed to the concessionaires the right to retain out of income or receive back from Government directly or as a credit, a sum free from all present or future taxes which shall be equal to 50% of net profits. In guaranteeing to the concessionaires 50% of net profits, these agreements appear to be in line with the 50-50 rule.

The principle of a 50% tax on net income was also applied in the concession agreement made between the Jordanian Government and John Mecom on March 25, 1964. In accordance with the terms of the agreement, the concessionaire undertook to pay income tax in accordance with the Jordanian Income Tax Law as amended on April 27, 1964. This amendment imposed a tax of 50% on the taxable income of any person or corporation engaged in the extraction, sale, disposition or export of petroleum substances or other hydrocarbons, provided that any royalty, tax or share paid to the Government with respect to such substances shall be deducted from the amount of the tax. Save for the royalty and income tax, the total of which amounts to 50% of taxable income, the concessionaire was granted a comprehensive exemption from all taxes and duties.

In addition to providing for a 50% share of profits either in the form of an income tax or a straight division of profits, certain concessions have coupled the income tax liability or the profit sharing obligation with a minimum financial consideration. Such minimum payment has taken the form either of a royalty or a tax payment. We have referred in the previous Section to cases where the royalty has a "floor", thus becoming a minimum payment. We shall now indicate the principal cases where in implementation of profit sharing arrangements concessions have provided for a minimum financial consideration in the form of a minimum payment.

(1) The earliest provision that envisaged a minimum to the concessionaire's payments to the Government was embodied in Iraq's agreement with the IPC group of companies made on February 3, 1952. The agreement stated that the Government's share in each year shall be not less than an amount equal to the value at posted prices of 25% of the net production of the Iraq company and the Mosul company respectively in that year, and of 33⅓% of the net production of the Basrah company in that year, in each case taking into account the value of royalty oil. The agreement further provided for a total minimum share in favour of the Government in the profits of the three companies: it stipulated that the companies undertake that the Government's share shall be not less than £.St. 20,000,000 per annum during the three following years and not less than £.St. 25,000,000 each year thereafter. Thus the minimum was expressed in terms of percentage of the value of exported production and also in terms of stated amounts.

(2) The agreement between the Ruler of Qatar and Shell Overseas Exploration Company (1952) stated that the Ruler's share of 50% of the "Oil Profit" shall be subject to a minimum of £650,000 a year.

(3) In accordance with the Kuwait-Shell agreement (1961), the company undertook that if in respect of any year after the date of commencement of regular exports of crude petroleum the Emir's receipts are at a rate less than the rate of £.St. 2,000,000 per annum, plus the amount of royalty paid or due, the company shall pay to the Emir a sum equal to the balance.

(4) The U.A.R.'s agreements with Phillips (1963) and with Pan American (1963 and 1964) all provided a "floor" to the receipts of the Government: they stated that the Government shall be entitled to receive in any tax year by way of royalty, rental and taxes 50% of the net profits realized by the concessionaire,

provided that the Government's receipts in any such year shall not be less than the value of the royalty.

(5) The Iranian Offshore agreements (1965) have provided that if the company's income tax liability is less than $12\frac{1}{2}\%$ of the value at posted price of its 50% share of the crude oil produced, then it shall make an additional payment to the Government which shall be equal to the deficiency.

B. EQUAL PROFIT SHARING

In some countries, the equal profit sharing concept was implemented by means of an agreement providing for a straight division of profits. This procedure was principally followed in Iraq and Qatar.

In Iraq, the equal sharing of profits between Government and concessionaire was introduced by an agreement made on February 3, 1952, amending the original conventions between Iraq and the IPC group of companies. Article 2 of the agreement stipulated that "the Government shall receive an amount equal to 50% of the profit resulting from the operations of the companies in Iraq." Such 50% of profit was made up of the $12\frac{1}{2}\%$ royalty, income tax and such amount which when added to the royalty and tax will be equal to the Government's share (Article 10).

On September 1, 1952, a somewhat similar agreement was made between the Ruler of Qatar and Petroleum Development Company whereby the company undertook that the Ruler shall receive an amount equal to 50% of the profits arising in Qatar on exported oil, less convention payments such as royalty and tax commutation.

The agreement made between the Ruler of Ras Al Khaima and Kuamco Oil in 1962 has envisaged the payment by the oil company to the Ruler of 50% of the "Oil Profit". The Oil Profit was defined as the difference between the aggregate income (ascertained on the basis of posted prices) and the cost of operations. The Ruler's 50% share of the "Oil Profit" is made up of an income tax and royalty which together with such makeup payment as may be required will equal 50% of the "Oil Profit".

The equal profit sharing concept was also applied in the Supplemental Agreement concluded on November 10, 1966 between the Ruler of Abu Dhabi and Abu Dhabi Marine Areas, Ltd.

C. INCOME SUBJECT TO INCOME TAX OR EQUAL PROFIT SHARING

The measure of the income accruing to the Governments under the profit sharing arrangements depends not only upon the rate of the tax or the percentage of sharing, as the case may be, but also on various other considerations relating to the manner of determination of gross income, net taxable income, deductible expenses and tax subtractions.

Before the introduction of the profit sharing concept the Governments of the producing countries were not concerned with the prices at which the concessionaire sold the crude oil nor with the concessionaire's profits or expenses. Even when the equal profit sharing arrangements were introduced in the fifties many matters which affect the determination of the income and the resulting income tax or sharing were left without precise definition or clarification. As a result, differences arose between the parties with regard to the prices of crude oil, discounts to buyers and allowable costs.

The price at which the crude oil is sold constitutes the measure of the concessionaire's gross income for income tax purposes. The manner of measuring gross income varied in the past by reason of the use of different methods, e.g.: the method of measuring income with reference to realized prices has been followed in Saudi Arabia and Libya; the method of using posted prices was applied in Iraq and Iran; measuring income with reference to weighted average of sale prices was in force in Bahrain (Bahrain-Bapco agreement of December 8, 1952), while weighted average prices received from non-affiliated customers were the basis adopted in Kuwait (Kuwait-KOC agreement of May 14, 1955).

All these methods for measuring the gross income of oil companies for income tax purposes have now been reduced to two: posted prices and realized prices.

Posted prices are the prices published by oil companies for FOB sales at a seaboard terminal in single cargo lots. It seems that posted prices first became a criterion of the income of oil companies by the agreement made in 1952 between Iraq and the IPC group of companies. Such criterion was subsequently applied in the Consortium's agreement with Iran in 1954 and was adopted by the Iranian Petro-

leum Act and oil agreements concluded thereunder. The Iranian
Petroleum Act required an oil operator to publish posted prices for
petroleum in respect of the relevant point of export and stated that
the gross receipts of each operator shall equal the value at applicable
posted prices of all petroleum exported by such operator (Article 11).
The criterion of posted prices was subsequently followed in Kuwait
and other countries.

Exceptionally, certain agreements have based the calculation of
profits on "border values" instead of posted prices. Such language is
found in concessions granted to the IPC group of companies or to
IPC subsidiaries. For example, the formula for calculating profits in
the Iraq-IPC agreement (1952) was based upon adjusted Iraq border
values. Profits in relation to crude oil exported meant the difference
between the Iraq border value and actual costs. Similarly in the
agreement between Qatar and Shell Overseas Exploration Company
(1952) the expression "profit arising in Qatar on exported oil" meant
the difference between the border value per ton of the exported oil
and the cost per ton of such oil multiplied by the number of tons so
exported. The same provision is found in the agreement between
Qatar and Qatar Petroleum Development Company (1952). However, border values are merely technical variations inspired, in the
case of IPC, by the fact that its production is transported by pipeline
and sold at published prices FOB a Mediterranean port rather than
at a domestic port. Border values are based upon posted prices and
changes in border values are directly related to, and governed by,
changes in posted prices.

The second basis for measuring the gross income of oil companies
is realized prices. Oil companies do not always sell at posted prices.
Generally, the posted price is a spot price for single cargo sales.
Volume sales to other than affiliates are in some cases discounted substantially with the result that the actual prices realized are less than
posted prices. The practice of relating gross income to realized prices
has been in application principally in Libya, the U.A.R. and Algeria.[9a]

[9a] In Saudi Arabia Aramco accounted to the Government until 1966 for
income tax purposes on the basis of posted prices in respect of sales to
affiliates and on the basis of realized prices in respect of sales to non-affiliated
purchasers. By the agreement concluded on September 30, 1966 between Saudi
Arabia and Aramco the practice of accounting on a realization basis in the
case of third party sales was abandoned and the company undertook to bill
its offtakers on the basis of published prices reduced only by the marketing

In 1965, Libya abandoned realized prices in favour of posted prices as a measure of the gross income of oil companies.[10]

The U.A.R. adopted realizations as the basis of income subject, however, to certain reservations. In the agreement with Phillips (1963), gross income is defined to mean amounts actually realized by Phillips or EGPC from sales of petroleum. If petroleum is sold to an affiliated company, as defined in the agreement, such petroleum shall be deemed to have been disposed of for a realized price determined in the same manner as that provided for the valuation of Government royalty. It will be recalled that the value of Government royalty is calculated on the basis of the weighted average export price received for crude oil by EGPC or Phillips from non-affiliated purchasers during the period for which such royalty is due, such price to be computed back to the field main storage tank. The same provisions occur in the U.A.R.'s agreement with Pan American of 1963 and 1964.

The Sahara Petroleum Code (1958) defined net taxable profits as the difference between the value of assets at the close of the fiscal year and those at the opening of the same year calculated in accordance with the rules mentioned in Article 64 of the Code. Thus, the tax is not limited to net operating results, but includes the net variation in value, if any, of capital assets.

Since the conclusion of the Franco-Algerian Agreement on Hydrocarbons (1965) there exists a third method for measuring the gross income of oil companies for tax purposes: the "value of reference".[11] This method, however, is peculiar to Algeria and is not of general application. The "value of reference" is based upon an average of prices published in Algeria before July 1, 1965; in effect, it is higher than previous prices actually realized but not quite as high as posted prices. Such "value of reference" will remain in effect until 1969 when the two Governments will examine whether, in the light of competitive factors, freight differentials and taxes in force, any alteration

---

allowances and the allowances established in accordance with the OPEC formula.

[10] The change was made by the Law of November 20, 1965 which amended the Libyan Petroleum Law (1955) and the current oil concessions were amended accordingly by agreements between the parties reached on January 20, 1966.

[11] The "value of reference" is defined in Articles 24 and 127 of the Franco-Algerian Agreement on Hydrocarbons, 1965.

should be made therein (Article 27). Realized prices will continue, however, to constitute the criterion for income tax purposes in the case of sales to the Algerian State for internal consumption or in the case of sales made at the request of the Algerian State under commercial agreements.

The problem presented by the prices of crude oil has not been limited to a choice between posted and realized prices for income tax purposes, but has extended to the price structure. Because posted prices are a major determinant of income and taxes on which the budgets of some Governments heavily depend,[12] the various Governments have become increasingly interested in participating in the determination of such prices. This matter has been under contention between OPEC countries and the oil companies since 1962. However, the agreements reached at the end of 1964 between oil companies and most OPEC countries with regard to the expensing of royalties have also settled this issue for the past: the agreements have recognized the propriety of the posted prices which have served as a basis for the determination of the income and income tax liability of the oil companies until their date.

Another issue which arose with respect to the measure of the income of oil companies for income tax purposes was the question of price discounts granted by them to the buyers of the oil. The practice as to discounts varied among oil producing countries. The Libyan law was the most liberal in this respect: it recognized the propriety of discounts on sales of crude oil provided that they were commercially fair and reasonable in relation to current market prices. In most other countries, no legislation or formal agreement existed with respect to the grant of discounts. The matter of discounts has been in issue with OPEC since 1962. By the agreements reached at the end of 1964 with most OPEC countries, it was agreed that the oil companies may account for tax purposes on the basis of certain declining discounts—described as allowances—off posted prices, such discounts to be applicable during a period of three years subject to their being reconsidered after its expiration in the light of changes in the economic, competitive and market situation of crude oil compared with such situation in 1964. It has been suggested that the aforementioned

---

[12] See Appendix II-D as to the proportion of oil revenue to total Government revenue in some oil producing countries in the Middle East.

arrangements were designed to achieve the financial effect of a partial expensing of royalties rather than settle the issue of realized prices versus posted prices. At its conference held in April 1966, OPEC recommended to member countries to take steps towards the complete elimination of the allowances granted to the oil companies

In addition, the same agreements confirmed a previously agreed upon marketing allowance equal to one-half (1/2) U.S. cent per barrel of crude oil exported.

By its Law of November 20, 1965, Libya withdrew its previous latitude with regard to discounts and followed the OPEC formula in this respect (Article VII).

Notwithstanding that posted prices are, subject to a few exceptions, generally the basis for measuring the income of oil companies for income tax purposes in the Middle East, OPEC adopted a resolution in April 1966 recommending to member countries to apply posted prices or reference prices for the purpose of determining the tax liabilities of the oil companies. The same resolution also recommended that no petroleum rights be granted or contracts be made by member countries concerning the exploration or exploitation of new areas unless royalty payments and income tax liabilities are calculated on the basis of posted or reference prices or unless the share to be obtained by the Government is not less favourable than that obtained under the existing arrangements based on posted or reference prices.

D. DEDUCTIBLE EXPENSES

The calculation of taxable profits is also affected by various considerations relating to costs, expenses and amortization. The original profit sharing arrangements were not sufficiently clear or specific on certain points in this regard. Problems that arose in practice were solved by subsequent agreements. No attempt will be made to refer to the various provisions governing deductible expenses as they appear in oil agreements or petroleum legislations. It will be sufficient to mention a few representative examples and to refer to certain general principles and practices.

Iraq's agreement with IPC (1952) laid down certain figures as fixed costs to be applied for the purpose of calculating the profit. These fixed costs were to be maintained from year to year unless and until actual costs differed from the fixed costs by more than 10%. In that event the actual costs were to be applied and maintained as fixed costs unless and until another variation of more than 10% occurred.

The Consortium's agreement[13] (1954) provided in Schedule II that in the computation of net income for income tax purposes the following items shall be deductible:

(1) The costs to the company of goods sold or services rendered by the company in connection with the carrying on of its operations in Iran;

(2) Expenses incurred by the company in connection with the carrying on of its operations in Iran, including, without in any way limiting the generality of the foregoing, administrative, overhead and establishment expenses; contributions and rents or other charges for the use of any property;

(3) The amount equal to any stated payment[14] or any other payment of a similar nature by the company in respect of crude oil, or, in the event crude oil is delivered in lieu of any such payment, the value, at the applicable posted price less any allowance applicable thereto, of the crude oil so delivered;

(4) A reasonable amount in each year for depreciation, obsolescence, exhaustion and depletion for the amortization of capital expenditure made by the company in connection with its operations in Iran; and

(5) Losses sustained in connection with the carrying on of the operations of the company in Iran and not compensated for by insurance or otherwise, including without in any way limiting the generality of the foregoing, bad debts, losses arising out of claims for damages against the company and losses resulting from damage to or the destruction or loss of stock-in-trade or any property used in connection with the said operations in Iran.

Subsequent oil agreements made by Iran which envisaged the payment of a bonus, such as the agreement with Pan American (1958) and the Offshore agreements (1965), have provided that the com-

---

[13] As amended by the Supplemental Agreement made in January 1965 with respect to the expensing of royalties.

[14] It will be recalled that the "stated payment" in Iran is equivalent to the royalty in other oil producing countries.

pany may also subtract from gross receipts during each of the ten taxable periods following the date of commercial production an amount equivalent to 10% of the total bonus paid by the company.

Kuwait's agreement with Shell (1961) provided that the cost of operations deductible from aggregate income shall be the total of the costs and expenses, as ascertained by sound and consistent accounting principles, incurred by the company and fairly and properly attributable to the operations of the company in the exercise and performance of the company's rights and obligations within the concession area in the State of Kuwait and in the area of concessionary waters. Such costs and expenses include provision for the exhaustion, depreciation and obsolescence of properties used by the company for its operations and shall be ascertained in accordance with the provisions of the Kuwait Income Tax Decree, subject to certain variations mentioned in the agreement. Similar provisions regarding deductible expenses were included in Kuwait's supplemental agreement with Aminoil (1961).

Costs incurred outside the producing country may be deducted from gross income if such costs are properly attributable to the producing country. The rule applicable in such cases varies with the arrangements made between oil companies and producing countries. In certain cases, agreement is reached on a percentage of certain costs incurred outside the producing country which is considered as properly attributable to such country for income tax purposes.

Foreign taxes were at first considered as deductible expenses. For example, the Saudi Arabian Royal Decree of December 27, 1950 provided in Article 2 that income taxes paid or payable to any foreign country were to be subtracted from net operating income. This provision, however, was deleted by a Royal Decree promulgated in 1952. Subsequent concession agreements or petroleum legislation have provided that foreign income taxes shall not be allowed as deductions from income. Exceptionally, the agreement made between Saudi Arabia and Japan Petroleum Trading Company (1957) stated that the concessionaire may deduct from net income foreign income taxes paid or accrued on income derived solely from sources without Saudi Arabia: this provision, however, flows from the nature of this agreement which envisaged Government participation in the concessionaire's profits realized within or without Saudi Arabia or the Neutral

Zone. A similar provision was included in Saudi Arabia's agreement with Auxirap (1965).

Except in Libya, the depletion allowance is not recognized as a deductible item for income tax purposes. The Libyan Petroleum Law allowed the deduction of a depletion allowance equal to 25% of gross income but limited to 50% of the profits of the year. The 1961 amendment of the Libyan Petroleum Law discontinued this privilege with respect to concessions granted thereafter. The Sahara Petroleum Code of 1958, which in many respects was modelled upon the Libyan Petroleum Law, did not recognize the depletion allowance as such, but permitted a tax deferment for five years on an amount equal to 27.5% of the well-head value of quantities produced.[15] This arrangement, which amounted to a form of a temporary depletion allowance, was terminated by Article 26 of the Franco-Algerian Agreement on Hydrocarbons (1965).

Turning to amortization, we find that the provisions in this regard are not always uniform in petroleum legislation or concessions. A few examples will suffice to indicate the variations in the rules applicable to amortization, particularly with respect to exploration expenses. Saudi Arabia's agreement with Japan Petroleum Trading Company (1957) provided that direct expenses of exploration and expenditures having the character of an investment of a permanent character shall be capitalized and not deducted from the gross operating income for the purpose of determining the net income. Kuwait's agreement with Arabian Oil Company (1958) stated that survey and exploration costs and a reasonable proportion of the indirect expenses incurred in field and development operations shall be treated as capital expenditure and shall not be included in the total costs and expenses save that an amount not exceeding 10% of such costs and expenses incurred after the commencement of regular exports may be so included until fully written off. Similar provisions were included in Kuwait's agreements with Shell (1961) and Aminoil (1961). Taking the agreement with Phillips (1963) as representative of the practice in this respect in the U.A.R., we note the provision therein that administrative and general expenses relating to exploration activities shall be capitalized and apportioned to the various investment items

---

[15] The amount on which tax was deferred was called *"fonds de reconstitution des gisements"*: see Articles 64 and 66 of the Code.

while such expenses as related to development and production activities shall be deducted from current income. The amortization of exploration expenditures as well as administrative and general expenses allocated to exploration shall be calculated using the straight line method over a period of five years.

The agreement made between Saudi Arabia and Aramco in 1963 laid down detailed provisions regarding the accumulation and deduction of exploration and intangible development costs. The former are to be amortized at a rate of 5% per annum while the latter are to be amortized at a rate of 10% per annum, provided that such costs, insofar as they relate to any relinquished area, shall, after being reduced by deductions already taken, be fully deductible in the year of such relinquishment.

While allowing amortization on exploration and development expenses incurred by the concessionaire during the exploitation period, the recent agreement between Saudi Arabia and Auxirap (1965) did not permit the deduction of exploration expenses incurred before the discovery of oil in commercial quantities.

The Iranian Offshore agreements (1965) stated that the company may subtract from its gross receipts during each taxation period in respect of amortization of all exploration expenditure an amount equal to one-fifteenth of that expenditure or U.S. $0.10 for each barrel of oil produced and saved, whichever is greater.

E. OFFSETS AGAINST INCOME TAX

Tax subtractions are always the subject of an express provision either in the tax or petroleum law or in the concession agreement. The first law which instituted a 50% income tax on the income of oil companies, namely the Saudi Arabian Royal Decree of December 27, 1950, authorized the subtraction from the income tax payable thereunder of the total of all taxes (except the income tax imposed by the Decree), royalties, rentals, duties and all other sums paid or payable to the Government. If the total of the foregoing exceeded 50% of the net operating income, then the excess shall be subtracted from the income tax which would otherwise be payable for the same taxable year (Article 3).

This principle was followed in subsequent tax laws and oil agreements. For example, the Decree issued in 1951 by Kuwait which imposed a 50% income tax on the income of oil companies stated that all taxes (other than the tax imposed by the Decree), royalties, rentals, duties, imposts and other exactions of a like nature which accrued or were received by the Ruler of Kuwait in the taxable year shall be credited against the 50% tax.

Such was also the position under the Libyan Petroleum Law of 1955 (Article 14) and in the Iranian Income Tax Act.[16] The Iranian agreements with AGIP, Pan American and Sapphire expressly provide that the payment of one half of the net profits to the Government shall expressly include any royalty, taxes and imposts for the account of the State and other public bodies.

However, since the recent agreements reached with some OPEC countries, royalties on crude oil up to 12½% of posted prices have ceased to be tax subtractions and can only be expensed. This is now the rule applicable in Saudi Arabia, Iran, Qatar and Libya.

New agreements expressly provide for the expensing of royalties. Thus, Saudi Arabia's agreement with Auxirap (1965) states that royalties shall be deductible as expenses.

Rents paid by the concessionaire are usually credited against the 50% tax. However, this rule is not invariable and is subject to certain exceptions:

(1) The agreement made on November 29, 1952 between Qatar and Shell Overseas Exploration Company provided that rent was to be excluded from the definition of convention payments: this meant in effect that rents could not be credited against the Ruler's 50% share of profits.

(2) The Iranian Petroleum Act (1957) allows rents to be credited against income tax under certain conditions. The Act provides that an operator may include the annual rental as part of his operating costs until such time as the income tax liability of the operator in any taxation period before taking into account the rental payment equals or exceeds the rental payment. Whenever in any taxation period the operator's tax liability equals or exceeds the rental payment, the rental shall not during that period be deducted from operating costs but shall instead be

---

[16] Article 35 of the Iranian Income Tax Act (1949) permits deduction from the income tax payable by oil companies of any "stated payment" or any other payment of a similar nature.

deemed to be the equivalent of a "stated payment" for the purposes of Article 35 of the Income Tax Act of 1949 and hence deductible from the income tax due by such operator (Article 9).

(3) The Egyptian practice allows rental payments, under certain conditions, to be credited against the royalty. The agreements with Phillips and Pan American provide that if the royalty during any year on production of petroleum from any lease exceeds one half of the total rent paid on the blocks converted into a development lease, such one half of the rent shall be refunded or, at the payer's election, shall be credited against the royalty or rent due from such party for the next succeeding year.

(4) Under Saudi Arabia's agreement with Auxirap (1965), rental payments are deductible as expenses, but rental payments made before the discovery of oil in commercial quantities are not deductible.

F. TAX COMMUTATION PAYMENTS

We have previously mentioned that it was the practice in early oil concessions in the Middle East to exempt the concessionaire from all taxation, though in certain cases taxes were commuted in consideration of fixed payments. For example, AIOC's concession (1933) provided in Article 11 that the company shall be exempt with respect to its operations in Persia for the first 30 years from any taxation, present or future, in consideration of the payment during the first 15 years of 9 pence per ton for the first 6,000,000 tons and 6 pence per ton in excess of 6,000,000 tons, with a guaranteed annual minimum of £.St. 225,000. During the 15 years following, the payments were to be increased to 1 shilling per ton for the first 6,000,000 tons and to 9 pence per ton in excess thereof, with a guaranteed annual minimum of £.St. 300,000. It was further agreed that before the year 1963 the parties shall come to an agreement as to the amounts of the annual payments to be made in consideration of the complete exemption of the company for its operations in Persia from any taxation during the remaining period of the concession.

The agreement made in 1937 between the Sultan of Muscat and Oman and Petroleum Concessions Ltd. provided for the company's right to import and export free of customs or export duty and taxes and for the exemption of the company, its personnel, operations, income and property from taxation in consideration of the payment, in addition to the royalty, of 4 annas per ton of petroleum won and saved. A similar provision was included in the Abu Dhabi concession of 1939.

In contrast with other concessions of that period, the original IPC concession from Iraq (1925) did not envisage, as already observed, the company's exemption from taxation. However, by an exchange of letters dated March 24, 1931, it was provided that the company shall be exempt from all taxation of whatever nature, whether State or municipal, on its capital, plant, machinery, buildings (other than houses and offices within municipal limits) and profits in consideration of a yearly payment of £.St. 9,000 gold to be increased to certain agreed amounts after the commencement of regular exports. In 1952, when IPC's convention was amended to provide for the equal sharing of profit, it was expressly stated that the Government shall receive in addition from each of the three companies concerned a tax commutation payment of £.St. 20,000 per annum.

KOC's agreement (1934) also provided for a tax exemption of the company's operations, income, profits and property and in consideration thereof the company undertook to pay to the Sheikh four annas per ton of petroleum on which royalty is payable. It may be remarked that when this agreement was revised in 1951 to provide for equal profit sharing, it specifically retained the tax commutation payment mentioned in the original concession.

The agreement made between Qatar and Petroleum Development Company in 1952 provided that in consideration of the payment by the company of a comprehensive taxation commutation amounting to a sum equal to 6 pence per ton of oil exported, the company shall be entitled:

(1) To import free of all import, customs and other duties, equipment, materials and goods required by the company or by its employees for its operations;

(2) To supply imported bunkers and other imported petroleum products to the company's ships or to any ship loading substances produced by the company and to export all substances free of all export customs or other duties;

(3) To exemption from all taxation of whatever nature

whether State or municipal and whether already imposed or here-
after to be imposed on its operations, capital, income, profits, bor-
ings, plants and properties, whether owned by the company or on
lease from any person, and on substances before and after removal
from the ground.

A similar tax commutation and exemption is found in the agreement made between Qatar and Shell Overseas Exploration Company
(1952).

G. TAX EXEMPTIONS AND TAX LIMITATIONS

With the introduction since mid-century of income taxes on the
profits of oil companies, the practice of stipulating tax commutation
payments in consideration of tax exemptions was abandoned, but
tax commutation payments already envisaged in old concessions were
retained. Similarly, the comprehensive tax exemption of which we
have seen examples in the early concessions was also abandoned in
favour of more qualified tax exemption provisions which were more
in the nature of tax limitations.

The limitation provisions are of an extreme variety. Taxes vary
from one country to another and it is not possible without going into
great detail to present a complete picture of tax limitations under
oil concessions. However, even at the risk of oversimplification it
might be of some use to extract some general principles and summarize tax exemptions and tax limitations in broad outline. An
examination of the fiscal provisions relating to oil concessions shows
that in respect of tax exemptions and tax limitations a distinction
exists between the following taxes, duties and fees:

(1) Income taxes on profits.

We have seen that all oil concessions now provide for the
payment to the producing country of an income tax or some
other sum which is measured by oil production profits. Such
obligation is coupled with a limitation laid down in the concession or in the relevant legislation intended to ensure that the
income tax or other payment shall not exceed a prescribed rate.[17]

(2) Import and export duties.

---

[17] In some recent concessions the concessionary company has submitted
to taxation without any limitation on the tax rate. These concessions will be
mentioned in the next subsection.

All concessions and oil legislations[18] invariably embody an exemption from import duties on equipment, materials and goods required for oil operations and from export duties on the petroleum or other products exported.

(3) Taxes and duties other than income taxes or import and export duties.

Here the practice varies considerably. In some cases, there exists a complete exemption of all such taxes or duties or a specific exemption of certain specified taxes and duties.[19] In other cases, although no tax exemption is expressly laid down and on the contrary the concessionaire is made subject to taxation generally applicable to other persons, a tax limitation incorporated in the law or the concession enables the concessionaire to credit any such taxes paid against the tax due on profits.[20] In a third kind of case, though the concessionaire may be exempted from taxes (related to profits) in excess of the rate prescribed in the law or the concession, such concessionaire is nonetheless required to pay other taxes and duties of general application, subject to a limitation on any increase in such taxes and duties over a certain level or percentage related to a date fixed in the law or the concession. Thus, Article 67 of the Sahara Petroleum Code stated

[18] See, for example, Article 16 of the Libyan Petroleum Law, Article 11 of the Iranian Petroleum Act and Article 68 of the Sahara Petroleum Code.

[19] Thus, Article 11 of the Iranian Petroleum Act stated in subsection G that

"Except for income tax payments and credits to be made to the National Iranian Oil Company pursuant to this Act, customs duties as limited by this Act, payment to Iran of taxes required to be withheld with respect to salaries paid to personnel and payments to contractors or agents for work carried out in Iran, non-discriminatory charges and fees for services rendered by the Government on request or to the public generally and non-discriminatory taxes and fees of general application (such as documentary stamp taxes, civil and commercial registry fees and patent and copyright fees), no operator shall be required to make any payment to any governmental authority whether central or local and no taxes shall be imposed on exports of petroleum by an operator nor on dividends paid by an operator from income arising as a result of its operations."

The principle embodied in Article 11 has been modified in the recent Iranian Offshore agreements as will be seen later.

[20] See, for example, Article 14 of the Libyan Petroleum Law.

that if by reason of changes in the basis of taxation or in tax rates or as a result of the creation of new taxes and duties, the burden on a concessionary company resulting from taxes and duties—other than the royalty and the tax which together total an amount equal to 50% of its profits—exceeds by 50% the burden of such taxes and duties as they existed at the date of the coming into force of the Code, the excess shall be credited against the tax on profits and, in the event of insufficiency, shall be credited against the royalty. This rule is not applicable, however, to taxes or payments for services rendered.[21] Subject to certain modifications, the same provision was substantially reproduced in Article 139 of the Protocol annexed to the Franco-Algerian Agreement on Hydrocarbons (1965).[22]

(4) Taxes and fees for services rendered by the Government or administrative authorities.

No exemption exists in respect of taxes and fees of general application which are in the nature of payments for services rendered by the Government of the producing country or by other administrative authorities. Thus, Article 28 (5) of the Consortium's agreement with Iran provided for the payment of:

"Charges and fees for services rendered by governmental authorities on request or to the public generally, such as tolls, water rates, sanitary and sewage charges, provided such charges and fees are reasonable and non-discriminatory."

This principle is now one of general application and has been laid down either in express terms[23] or has been tacitly accepted in practice.

It is apparent that most oil concessions embody some kind of tax limitation in one form or another, either with respect to taxation generally over and above a certain tax rate or a tax level or with respect to specific taxes and duties. Three forms of tax limitation

---

[21] *Journal Officiel de la République Française,* November 23, 1958, p. 10534.

[22] *Journal Officiel de la République Française,* December 26, 1965 p. 11812.

[23] See, for example, Article 11 of the Iranian Petroleum Act, Article 67 of the Sahara Petroleum Code and Article 139 of the Protocol annexed to the Franco-Algerian Agreement on Hydrocarbons (1965).

may be briefly mentioned: the tax ceiling, the guarantee against future tax increases and the guarantee of the concessionaire's share of the profits.

THE TAX CEILING

The most common form of tax limitation is the tax ceiling. Such limitation is achieved either by means of a contractual or a statutory provision or both. Thus, the Royal Decree issued by the Government of Saudi Arabia on December 27, 1950 which imposed an income tax on the profits of oil companies limited such tax to 50% of the net operating income. The same limitation was incorporated in the agreement concluded between Aramco and the Government of Saudi Arabia on December 30, 1950 whereby the company submitted to this tax. Similarly, the Consortium's agreement with Iran enumerated certain taxes and payments due to the Government and NIOC and then declared that the Consortium members, their Trading Companies and their Operating Companies shall be free of all other taxation. The same principle was incorporated in Article 11 of the Iranian Petroleum Act. Article 14 of the Libyan Petroleum Law and concessions granted thereunder have also limited the total amount of the fees, rents, royalties[24] and taxes payable by the concession holder to 50% of annual profits. The provisions contained in the Sahara Petroleum Code and the Protocol annexed to the Franco-Algerian Agreement on Hydrocarbons which limit the fiscal burden arising from taxes and duties other than the tax on profits to a certain level were noted earlier. With the exception of certain agreements recently concluded in Iran, Arabia and Algeria presently to be mentioned, all concessions embody a ceiling which limits taxation on income to the level fixed in the law or the agreement.

GUARANTEE AGAINST FUTURE TAX INCREASES

Some agreements and legislations have not only set a ceiling on the taxes to be levied on the income of oil companies but have also

---

[24] As mentioned earlier, royalties are not taken into account since 1965 in determining the 50% of annual profits which are payable to the Government.

given what may be described as a fiscal guarantee against any future income tax increase or against other impositions. Such guarantee was given in Iran and Algeria.

The Consortium's agreement (1954) stated that Iran undertook that throughout the term of the agreement the provisions of law and the rates of income tax governing the income tax liability of the Trading and Operating Companies in Iran shall be not less favourable to them than the provisions and rates in the law existing on August 1, 1954, as amended by the agreement (Article 28). This principle was given general application by the Iranian Petroleum Act. Article 11 of the Act provided that every operator shall, with respect to his net income, be subject to taxation in accordance with prevailing income tax laws, provided, however, that the rates of income tax governing the Iranian income tax liability of the operator shall not exceed the rates prescribed in the Income Tax Act of 1956. The Act also stated that each operator shall, with respect to his net income, be entitled to provisions not less favourable than those established in Article 35 of the Income Tax Act of 1949 as preserved in Article 36 of the Income Tax Act of 1956.

However, the recent Iranian Offshore agreements (1965) have abandoned the principle of tax limitation laid down in the Petroleum Act but have envisaged a new kind of tax guarantee. The agreements stated that with respect to their income tax liability the parties and any Trading Companies are subject to taxation in accordance with the Iranian income tax laws as they may prevail from time to time. However, the Government of Iran guarantees that the parties and any Trading Companies shall not be subject to rates of income tax or other provisions governing net income which are less favourable than those applicable to other companies engaged in similar operations producing more than 50% of Iranian crude oil.[25] The significance of this provision will be discussed in the next subsection.

The Sahara Petroleum Code (1958) combined tax limitations with a guarantee against non-aggravation of the fiscal position of the concessionary company. In addition to fixing a tax rate which, in-

---

[25] See Article 30 in the Shell-NIOC, Tidewater-NIOC and other Iranian Offshore agreements of January 16, 1965. The same provision occurs in Article 30 of the Iranian Offshore agreement with a German group of companies dated June 16, 1965.

clusive of the royalty, was equal to 50% of the taxable profit (Article 65) and to limiting the increase in the incidence of other taxes and duties to 50% over their level at the date of the coming into force of the Code (Article 67), the Code guaranteed that its fiscal provisions will not be "aggravated" during the period of the search permit and also during a period of 25 years from the date of the concessions granted thereunder, provided that the total period of the guarantee shall not exceed 30 years (Article 70).[26] The Explanatory Statement to the Code mentioned that the substantial amounts required for investment and the uncertainties inherent in such investment justify the giving of guarantees of stability to national and foreign investments. The two tax limitations embodied in the Sahara Petroleum Code with respect to the tax on profits and the incidence of other taxes and duties have, subject to certain modifications, been reproduced in the Protocol annexed to the Franco-Algerian Agreement on Hydrocarbons (1965) with regard to companies whose activities it regulates (Articles 125 and 139) but the guarantee against non-aggravation of the concessionaire's fiscal position has been omitted.

GUARANTEE OF THE CONCESSIONAIRE'S PROFITS

The practice of the U.A.R. with respect to tax limitation is different from practices followed elsewhere. The only tax exemption which is expressly included in oil concession agreements concerns customs taxes and duties. The tax limitation designed to secure the preservation of the 50% income tax rate is attained indirectly by means of other provisions. The agreement made with Phillips (1963) provided that the Government shall receive in any tax year by way of royalty, rent and taxes (including income taxes) 50% of the net profits realized and received by the operator. On the other hand, the agreement embodied a guarantee that the operator will receive in every tax year a sum free from all present and future taxes (including income taxes) which shall be equal to 50% of the net profits for such tax year. The two agreements made with Pan American in 1963 and 1964 similarly stated that the Government guarantees that during every year of the term of the agreement Pan American shall have the

---

[26] *Journal Officiel de la République Française,* November 23, 1958, p. 10527.

right to receive and to retain abroad, free from all present and future taxes, imposts and any other exactions and payments required by the U.A.R., a sum equal to 50% of its net profits.

H. INCOME TAXES IN EXCESS OF 50% OF NET PROFITS OR UNEQUAL PROFIT SHARING

Although the principle of the equal division of profits received widespread application in the Middle East and North Africa, a few agreements have deviated from it and have embodied an income tax rate in excess of 50% of net profits or have provided for unequal profit sharing. These agreements are reviewed hereinafter.

The 50-50 rule was first breached in 1957 by the agreement concluded between Saudi Arabia and Japan Petroleum Trading Company, subsequently named the Arabian Oil Company. The agreement provided for payment of income taxes in accordance with the Income Tax Decree of November 1950, as amended in 1956,[27] which prescribes an income tax rate of 40%. The agreement further stipulated that if the royalties and taxes received by the Government do not amount to 56% of the company's net income, the company shall pay to the Government "an additional income tax" so as to bring up the Government's receipts to 56% of the company's net income (Article 14). The law of Saudi Arabia does not provide for an income tax rate of 56% nor does it contain any provision regarding the payment or imposition of an additional income tax. Such tax, therefore, must be considered to be in the nature of a contractual obligation rather than a statutory fiscal imposition. Saudi Arabia's agreement with Auxirap (1965) followed a different line: it stated that the concessionaire shall pay on its integrated operations the income taxes imposed by the "relevant" Saudi Arabian laws and decrees now existing or which may later exist during the life of the agreement (Article 22). As income tax rates in Saudi Arabia do not at present exceed

---

[27] In Saudi Arabia, there exist at present two income tax Decrees:

(a) The Income Tax Decree of November 4, 1950, as amended in 1956, imposes a progressive income tax on the net profits of companies starting at a rate of 20% and reaching a rate of 40% on taxable income exceeding one million riyals.

(b) The Income Tax Decree of December 27, 1950 imposes an income tax of 50% of the net operating income of companies engaged in the production of petroleum or other hydrocarbons.

50% of net profits, Auxirap's concession does not strictly speaking deviate in practice from the 50-50 rule. Its only particularity is the absence therein of any tax limitation.

The agreement made by Kuwait with Arabian Oil Company (1958) also breached the 50-50 rule by its provision that Kuwait will receive 57% of the "Oil Profit" (to be ascertained on the basis of posted prices) and 57% of the "Marketing Profit" (Article 7).

The Supplemental Agreement made between Kuwait and Aminoil (1961) which revised the original agreement provided that the company will pay to the Emir the greater of 50% of the "Oil Profit" (ascertained on the basis of posted prices) or 57% of the "Oil Income" (ascertained on the basis of realizations). It is doubtful, however, whether this agreement does technically breach the 50-50 rule because, notionally at least, it respects the 50-50 rule on the basis of posted prices. It is only if 57% of realized prices is higher than 50% of posted prices that a breach of the 50-50 rule would occur.

The Hadramaut-Pan American concession (1961) also departed from the 50-50 rule. It provided that the two contracting Governments shall receive from the company an income tax of 55% of the company's net profits. The agreement further stated in the event that in any tax year the total amount of fees, rentals, royalties, income taxes and other taxes and imposts payable by the company to the Governments or any municipalities—excepting payments to the Governments for services rendered—is less than 55% of the company's net profits for such tax year, the company shall pay to the two Governments concerned a sum by way of an additional tax on income in an amount sufficient to make the total of its payments to the Governments equal to 55% of its net profit. The agreement stipulated, however, that if the Governments exercise the option given to them to acquire a 20% interest in the venture, the company shall be entitled by virtue of such participation to a tax credit which shall reduce from 55% to 50% the share of its net profits payable to the Governments. It follows that this concession is on a 50-50 basis with the two Governments' 20% participation in the enterprise or on a 55-45 basis without such participation.

The agreement made between the U.A.R. and Eastern Petroleum Company (1959) provided that the exploiter must pay all taxes and duties then in force or which will be in force in the future and which the exploiter is legally obliged to pay. The Government shall have the right to receive either the royalty on crude oil, rental, customs duties and taxes due by the company or by its shareholders on profits resulting from exploitation works, or an amount equal to 50% of the company's profits, whichever is higher.

The agreement made between the U.A.R. and ENI (1963) stated that the concessionaire shall pay, besides royalty and rentals, all taxes payable by industrial enterprises in general and the tax on dividends to shareholders. The Government shall be entitled to 50% of the net profits or to the aggregate of royalties, rentals and taxes, whichever is the higher. However, the agreement stated that notwithstanding the preceding provision, the Government undertakes that the foreign shareholders of the concessionaire representing 50% of its share capital shall every year have the right to a sum, free from all present and future taxes and duties, which shall be equal to 25% of the net profits resulting from the concessionaire's operations under the contract. On the basis of ENI's equity in the enterprise, this provision is equivalent to a guarantee to foreign shareholders of 50% of net profits free from all taxes.

The Iranian Offshore agreements (1965) have abandoned in principle the 50-50 rule. These agreements provided that the parties shall be subject to taxation on their net income in accordance with the Iranian Tax Laws as they may prevail from time to time. However, the Government of Iran guarantees that the parties shall not be subject to rates of income tax or other provisions governing net income which are less favourable than those applicable to other companies engaged in similar operations which together produce more than 50% of Iranian crude oil. The effect of this provision appears to be the following: since Iran's agreement with the Consortium (1954) lays down a tax ceiling of 50% and since the various companies forming the Consortium produce more than 50% of Iranian crude oil, the companies which are parties to the Iranian Offshore agreements will benefit from such tax ceiling during the life of the Consortium's agreement provided, of course, that the Consortium's production continues to exceed 50% of Iran's crude oil production.

Finally, the Franco-Algerian Agreement on Hydrocarbons (1965) has introduced new income tax rates in excess of 50% while leaving the income tax rate of 50% prescribed in the Sahara Petroleum Code

unaffected in certain cases. The result, therefore, is that there exist
at present in Algeria three income tax rates applicable to the profits
of oil companies. These rates apply as follows:

(1) a tax rate of 50% on the profits of companies which were
unaffected by the said Agreement, i.e., foreign companies;

(2) a tax rate of 50% rising progressively to 55% on the
profits of French companies (Article 23 of the Agreement);

(3) a tax rate of 55% on the profits of the French and Algerian companies envisaged by the Cooperative Association established under the Protocol annexed to the Agreement (Article
125 of the Protocol).

I. EXTRATERRITORIAL TAXATION AND INTEGRATION

The principle generally recognized in oil concessions in the
Middle East is that the 50% income tax on oil profits applies only to
profits realized on the territory of the conceding State. These usually
consist of oil production profits. This rule is either expressed by, or
implied from, the terms of the various concessions and agreements or
the applicable tax laws. In some cases, the agreements specifically provide that income taxes shall be paid on activities and operations conducted on the territory of the State. Another common way of limiting
geographically the application of income taxes is to relate the taxable
income to posted prices or border values. The principle of the territorial taxation of oil profits is in line with the general taxation systems
in force in the region, except the U.A.R. However, in its oil agreements, the U.A.R. observes the principle of territorial taxation of
profits.

An exception to the general pattern of territorial taxation of oil
profits is found in the agreements existing between the Arabian Oil
Company and Saudi Arabia and Kuwait with respect to the offshore
of the Neutral Zone outside territorial waters.[28] In addition to providing for a rate of tax in excess of 50%, these two agreements have
also adopted the concept of "integration" or Government's participation in "downstream" operations, i.e., refining, transportation and
marketing. The agreement between Saudi Arabia and Japan Petroleum Trading Company, subsequently assigned to the Arabian Oil

---

[28] The land area and territorial waters of the Neutral Zone fall within
the concessions held by Getty and Aminoil.

Company, stated that the company will carry out all its operations including production, refining, transportation and marketing as an integrated oil enterprise and will pay an income tax at the rate of 56% on all its operations inside and outside Saudi Arabia including sale of crude oil, refining, transportation and marketing. The agreement also provided that income derived from the operations of tankers is considered income derived partly within and partly without Saudi Arabia (Article 14). The same principles were incorporated in the agreement made by Kuwait and Arabian Oil Company in 1958 in respect of its undivided interest, except that the rate of tax was fixed at 57% (Article 7).

Saudi Arabia's agreement with Auxirap (1965) provided that once the operating company envisaged by the agreement is formed, the concessionaire will function as an integrated company, carrying out production, refining, transportation and marketing of crude oil (Article 26). The agreement also envisaged the taxing of profits arising from integrated operations within and outside Saudi Arabia.

The principle of Government participation in the profits resulting from integrated operations was not an innovation introduced by Saudi Arabia's agreements with Japan Petroleum Trading Company and Auxirap. Such principle had already been the subject of the agreement made on December 22, 1920 between the Persian Government and the Anglo-Persian Oil Company and which continued in operation until it was abandoned in 1933 in the circumstances already mentioned in Section 2 of Chapter I.

SECTION 6. ANCILLARY BENEFITS

Oil concessions often impose upon the concessionaire obligations which in some cases constitute ancillary advantages in favour of the producing country in addition to the financial benefits already considered. In other cases, such obligations are merely incidental to the employment of labour in desert areas and may not, in fact, represent a financial benefit to the producing country. The distinction between such obligations is not always made.

In the past, ancillary benefits were not numerous nor of much consequence. They consisted mainly of:

(1) An obligation to supply petroleum or products without charge or at reduced prices;

(2) An obligation to make certain loans to the Government;[29]

(3) Educational grants;[30]

(4) The grant to Government without payment on its part of a share in the oil company's capital stock.[31]

Towards mid-century a change occurred in the nature and number of ancillary benefits. Nowadays these benefits cover a variety of obligations relating to education, training of employees, medical services, scientific advancement, refining[32] and the supply of petroleum or petroleum products.

Concessionary provisions relating to ancillary benefits or obligations differ from one country to another. Some countries may be particularly interested in the construction of schools and the promotion of educational or medical facilities. Almost all countries insist upon the inclusion in oil concessions of an obligation with respect to the technical and industrial training of the concessionaire's personnel. A few illustrative provisions may be mentioned.

Aminoil's agreement with Kuwait (1948) imposed upon the company the obligations:

(1) To provide for its employees in the Neutral Zone all necessary medical services;

(2) Within four years after the date of discovery of petroleum to construct a modern dispensary and hospital containing 30 beds to be devoted primarily to the treatment of tuberculosis and similar diseases;

(3) In such event also to begin a program of education whereby financial assistance will be given to certain Kuwaiti

---

[29] e.g. as in Aramco's concession (1933).

[30] AIOC's concession made provision for a yearly educational grant of £.St. 10,000 and the Kuwait-KOC agreement (1951) stipulated a similar annual payment of £.St. 45,000.

[31] Two concessions have included such grant: D'Arcy's concession (£20,000 in paid-up shares) and Aminoil's concession (15% of the company's shares as well as 15% of the capital stock of the refinery). See further on this point Section 2 of Chapter IV.

[32] Refining obligations will be discussed in the following Chapter.

nationals by the company to attend schools and institutions of learning (Article 8).

A number of obligations relating to the erection and maintenance of schools and educational and training facilities were imposed on the concessionary company in Getty's concession from Saudi Arabia (1949).

Kuwait's agreement with Shell (1961) imposed upon the company the following ancillary obligations:

(1) To train and employ subjects of the Emir as far as practicable for all works in management and operations;

(2) To provide free of charge for its employees and for officials working in the concession area all necessary medical services including hospitalization, dispensary and clinical facilities;

(3) Effective from the discovery of oil in commercial quantities to prepare in consultation with the Emir a special program for higher education in university, technical college or equivalent institutions in Kuwait and abroad. It was stipulated that in any one year the number of trainees in such university, college and institution shall not be less than 15% of the total number of non-Arab staff in the employment of the company in the previous year;

(4) To establish in Kuwait all such laboratory and other research facilities as shall be appropriate to the company's operations and obligations under the agreement.

The Consortium's agreement with Iran did not require the Consortium members to provide directly any particular services though it laid upon them a part of the financial burden relating thereto. In accordance with the agreement, NIOC undertook to perform and carry out "non-basic operations". This term meant the provision, maintenance and administration of certain ancillary services to employees including essential services, like housing, food supply, transport, and also other services, such as medical and health services, industrial and technical training and education and welfare facilities. The cost of such services was divided into capital expenditure and operating expenses. The former is provided in equal parts by NIOC and the relevant Operating Company while the latter are borne in the first instance by NIOC subject to a refund by the relevant Operating

Company of such costs to NIOC to such extent as is reasonable. Other oil agreements made by Iran have imposed an obligation with respect to the technical and industrial training of Iranian personnel.

The Libyan Petroleum Law of 1955 imposed upon concessionaires the obligation as from the date of commencement of regular exports to make certain annual payments of not less than £.Lib. 2,500 and not more than £.Lib. 5,000 to be applied towards giving Libyan subjects technical training in the petroleum industry. The Libyan Petroleum Law, as amended in 1961, gave the applicant for an oil concession the liberty to include in his application particulars of any economic, financial and other benefits or advantages that he is willing to offer to the Government over and above the requirements of the Petroleum Law. In accordance with this provision, the various oil concessions granted by Libya during the summer of 1966 have embodied a number of ancillary benefits. Such benefits have included scholarships for Libyan students, production bonuses, expenditure commitments regarding exploration, a participation option in favour of the Government to the extent of 25% of the enterprise upon the discovery of oil and, in a few cases a 52% profit sharing arrangement in favour of the Government.[32a]

Almost all concessions have embodied provisions concerning the supply to the producing country of petroleum and petroleum products at reduced prices or in some cases without charge. Thus, AIOC's concession (1933) stipulated that sales to Government should be subject to 25% discount while sales to other consumers should be subject to 10% discount. Aramco's concession (1933) made provision for the supply of specified quantities of crude oil or products to the Government without charge. Getty's agreement with Saudi Arabia (1949) recognized Government's right to purchase for its own use up to 20% of petroleum and petroleum products subject to a 5% discount. The agreement made between Saudi Arabia and Japan Petroleum Trading Company (1957) stated that the Government shall have the right to purchase for its own use but not for resale for export an amount not exceeding 10% of the petroleum and petroleum products produced at the price at which same is sold to any other purchaser less a discount of 5%. The same provision occurs in the agreement made between Kuwait and the same company in 1958.

The Iranian Petroleum Act provided that NIOC shall require

[32a] See *Petroleum Press Service*, August 1966, p. 304.

each operator to undertake to deliver to it a portion of such petroleum as may be required for internal consumption at cost price plus a reasonable operating fee. However, no operator shall be required to produce at a rate higher than the maximum rate of efficient production or to supply quantities or qualities of petroleum disproportionate to that which may be required from other operators engaged in petroleum operations in Iran. These principles have been embodied in petroleum concessions granted by Iran.

The policy of the U.A.R. with respect to the purchase of petroleum or petroleum products has shown concern for its internal needs. Since the U.A.R. itself refines products needed for its own internal requirements but its own sources of production do not as yet fulfil its own needs, it generally includes in its oil agreements a provision for the purchase of a portion of the concessionaire's crude oil production. The agreement made between the U.A.R. and Eastern Petroleum Company (1959) reserved to the General Petroleum Organization a right of priority to purchase the crude oil and its refined products obtained from the exploited area subject to a reduction of 10% on the price of similar crude in a recognized world market and the minimum world price given in *Platt's Oilgram Bulletin* for products. These terms apply to 20% of the crude oil or its products refined in the U.A.R. The agreement made between the U.A.R. and Phillips (1963) gave the Government the right to purchase for refinery requirements in the U.A.R. in any year a portion of the oil produced by EGPC and Phillips as corresponds to the proportion which the oil so produced bears to the total quantity of crude oil produced in the U.A.R. during the same year. All crude oil purchased by the Government which is not in excess of a quantity equal to 20% of the crude oil produced and owned by EGPC or Phillips shall be at a price of 10% less than the weighted average price obtained by EGPC and Phillips for exported crude oil. Any crude oil purchased by the Government in excess of the said 20% shall be purchased either at the current price employed in computing royalties or at the weighted average export price actually received from third parties. Under its two agreements with Pan American made in 1963 and 1964, the U.A.R. reserved the right to purchase a quantity not exceeding 20% of the crude oil produced at a price of 10% less than the average price obtained for exported crude oil.

The North African oil concessions have also evidenced a concern

for the satisfaction of internal needs before exportation of the oil produced. Thus, the Sahara Petroleum Code stated that the concessionaires may be required to give priority to the supply of the franc zone,
after satisfaction of the internal consumption needs of the zones
comprised within the organization of the Sahara regions (Article 32).
The Tunisian Decrees of March 2, 1950 approving the conventions
granted to *Compagnie des Pétroles de Tunisie, Société Nord-Afri-
caine des Pétroles et Société de Recherches et d'Exploitation des
Pétroles en Tunisie (Serept)* embodied a commitment by the companies to reserve up to 60% of the oil produced for the needs of the
Tunisian economy, the prices of purchase being determined on the
basis of prices of imported products of the same nature. The convention made between the Tunisian Government and Conorada Petroleum Corporation (1958) reserved the right of the Tunisian State
to purchase 20% of the petroleum produced for its internal needs
at world prices subject to a discount of 10%. Similar obligations were
envisaged by the oil legislation of Morocco: the model book of conditions for oil concessions approved by the Decree of July 23, 1958
required, *inter alia,* the satisfaction of local needs prior to the exportation of the petroleum produced.

SECTION 7. THE EVOLUTION IN THE FINANCIAL CONSIDERATION OF OIL CONCESSIONS

After reviewing in the preceding Sections the financial conditions
of oil concessions, we are in a better position to perceive the general
evolution which has taken place in the consideration payable under
oil concessions, particularly since the middle of the century. This consideration has passed through three stages:

(1) The period prior to 1950 when a fixed cash royalty constituted the principal payment by the concessionaire under an
oil concession.

(2) The period from 1950 to 1965 when the consideration
consisted of the equal sharing of the profits calculated before the
deduction of the royalty and the royalty was treated as a part of
the producing country's share.

(3) The period since 1965 when equal sharing is based
upon the profits calculated after the deduction of royalties and

the royalty is payable in addition to the producing country's 50% share of the profits.

It is evident that the equal profit sharing concept though of recent origin has not remained static. Even though the income tax rate of 50% of net profits—which in its inception was designed to implement the equal sharing formula—was retained in most cases, the original equal sharing concept itself has been eroded by factors unconnected with the rate of the tax.

The first factor resulted from the recent arrangements concerning the expensing of the royalty. These arrangements have altered the respective percentages of the producing country and oil company in profit sharing. Such percentages now apparently stand in the ratio of 58% to Government and 42% to the oil company.[33]

The second factor is due to the gap which exists between realized and posted prices. In those countries where income tax is computed on the basis of posted prices regardless of the prices actually received, the ratio between Government and company income is affected to the detriment of the latter. This fact is significantly brought out by the agreement concluded between Kuwait and Aminoil in 1961. This agreement provided, it will be recalled, that Kuwait shall be entitled to the greater of 50% of the "Oil Profit" calculated on the basis of posted prices or 57% of the "Oil Income" ascertained on the basis of realized prices. It has even been suggested that a 50-50 division of profits based on posted prices may be equivalent to a 60-40 or even a 70-30 division based on realized prices.[34]

These two factors constituted inroads on the equal profit sharing concept as understood and implemented at mid-century. Nowadays, the concept has become more notional than real.

The evolution in the financial consideration of oil concessions has affected, as we have seen earlier, all concessions, old or new alike. Furthermore, such evolution has been accompanied by certain significant developments whose impact, however, was limited to new concessions. These developments were three in number.

First, new concessions were marked by a substantial increase in bonus payments, rents and ancillary benefits.

Secondly, the 50% limitation on the income tax rate on oil pro-

---

[33] *The Economist,* January 1965, p. 352.
[34] *Petroleum Press Service,* September 1963, p. 322.

duction profits was abandoned in some new concessions by the concessionaire undertaking to pay income taxes existing now or which may exist in the future. In most cases, however, as in the recent Iranian Offshore agreements and in Saudi Arabia's concession to Auxirap, the abandonment has been made in principle only because, in fact, the 50% rate has been maintained.

Thirdly, a large number of new concessions have envisaged a joint venture arrangement in oil production between the concessionaire and the producing country or its national oil company. Such arrangement enables the producing country to participate on a partnership basis in the oil enterprise and, in consequence, to increase its financial benefits. It has been suggested that such a joint venture arrangement is based upon a new sharing formula representing a Government-company ratio of 75-25 in net profits in lieu of the 50-50 sharing formula which has become obsolete. The true nature of the sharing formula applied in joint venture arrangements existing between oil companies and producing countries will be examined in Chapter IV hereinafter.

Chapter III

General Conditions of Oil Concessions

SECTION 1. ABANDONMENT OR SURRENDER BY CONCESSIONAIRE

As a rule concessions contain a provision enabling the concessionaire to abandon or surrender the concession. In recent years, however, this right has gradually been subjected to certain conditions and limitations.

The first oil concession granted in the Middle East in 1901 contained no provision for its abandonment by the concessionaire.

Iraq's concession to IPC (1925) reserved the company's right to abandon permanently to the Government all rights under the concession upon giving three months' notice. If such notice be given not later than 30 years after the date of the convention, the company shall be entitled to remove, free of all taxes and duties, all plant, buildings, stores, material and property of every sort provided that for a period of three months from the receipt of such notice the Government may purchase the same at a price equal to the replacement value at that time less depreciation (Article 38).

AIOC's concession gave the company the right to surrender the concession on giving to the Government two years' notice. On the expiration of the period of the notice, the company's property in Persia would become free of cost the property of the Government and the company would be released from any engagement for the future (Article 25).

Aramco's concession gave the company in Article 28 the right to terminate the contract by giving the Government thirty days' notice. Upon such termination the Government and the company will be free of all further obligations under the contract except as follows:

(1) Liability for any amounts due by the company to the Government and still unpaid remains unaffected;

(2) The company's immovable property becomes the property of the Government free of charge; and

(3) The company will afford the Government an opportunity to purchase its movable property in Saudi Arabia at a fair price equal to its replacement value at the time, less depreciation.

Article 12 of Kuwait's agreement with KOC gave the company the right, at any time after it has drilled 4,000 feet or after the expiry of two years from the date of signature, whichever shall be the later date, to terminate the agreement upon giving the Sheikh one year's notice. The company shall have no further liabilities except to pay all monies due to the Sheikh up to the date of termination. It was further provided that, in the event of termination within 35 years from the date of signature, all lands and buildings and other immovable property of the company within Kuwait shall be handed over to the Sheikh free of cost. If such termination occurred after 35 years, all the movable and immovable property of the company in Kuwait shall be handed over to the Sheikh free of cost. An identical provision as to surrender, subject to the same conditions and consequences, was contained in Kuwait's agreement with Aminoil.

Saudi Arabia's agreement with Pacific Western Oil Company stipulated that the company may abandon and relinquish its rights under the agreement by giving six months' notice to the Government, provided, however, that if the date fixed for abandonment and relinquishment is a date earlier than two years from the date of signature of the agreement, the payment of the aggregate amount of annual minimum royalties amounting to not less than U.S. $3,000,000 shall be a condition precedent to the exercise by the company of such right of abandonment and relinquishment. In the event of the termination of the agreement, either by mutual consent or by reason of abandonment or relinquishment by the company, the latter shall retain ownership of all movables and may remove same but all immovable property of the company within the Neutral Zone shall become the property of the Government (Article 46).

The Libyan Petroleum Law stated that the concession holder shall be entitled at any time, by giving three months' notice in writing to the Petroleum Commission,[1] to surrender the whole or any part of the concession area (Article 10).

The Iranian oil agreements do not, as a rule, envisage abandonment or surrender by the concessionaire. The Consortium's agreement provided that the agreement shall neither expire nor be terminated before its expiry except by mutual agreement or arbitration. Exceptionally, however, Iran's oil agreements since 1957 recognize the other party's right to abandon or surrender under certain conditions: it is clear that no abandonment can take place before the expiration of four years from the date of the agreement by reason of a condition stating that during the first four annual periods exploration operations may not be suspended or stopped for any reason whatsoever except *force majeure*; however, at the end of four years and of each of the following eight years, the other party may discontinue exploration operations and relinquish its rights after proving that up to the date of notification the exploration work planned to be carried out has in fact been carried out and that all amounts allocated for expenditure on exploration during the period prior to such notification have been fully spent; in the event that there remains an unexpended balance, one half of such balance shall be paid to NIOC. If no oil is discovered within a period of twelve years, the oil agreement terminates.

Saudi Arabia's agreement with Japan Petroleum Trading Company gave the company the right to abandon its concession upon giving the Government two months' notice during the exploration period and six months' notice during the exploitation period, or if the company pays to the Government one half of the Government's share of profits for the preceding year (Article 45). A similar provision occurs in Kuwait's agreement with the Arabian Oil Company. This agreement further provided that if it is terminated by the company not more than ten years from its date, all immovable property belonging to the company in Kuwait or the Neutral Zone shall vest in the Sheikh free of cost, but if such termination occurred more than ten years from the date of the agreement all movable and immovable properties of the company shall vest in the Sheikh free of cost.

Kuwait's agreement with Shell gave the company the right at any time after the third anniversary date to terminate the agreement upon

---

[1] The functions of the Petroleum Commission have now been taken over by the Ministry of Petroleum Affairs.

giving 60 days' notice; if such termination occurs within 25 years the company's immovable properties shall be handed over to the Emir; if such termination occurs after 25 years the Emir's right extends to both movable and immovable properties (Article 21).

The U.A.R. makes a distinction between the surrender of an exploration block and the surrender of a development lease. Its agreement with Phillips provided that, upon or at any time after the expiration of the third year after the effective date of the agreement, Phillips shall have the privilege at any time, upon 90 days' prior notice to the Government, to surrender any or all of the exploration blocks then held by it and upon such surrender shall be released and discharged from any and all further exploration and other obligations under the agreement provided that, if at the time of such surrender, exploration expenditures have aggregated less than the amounts required to be spent during the periods preceding such surrender, then an amount equal to one half of the difference between the amount that should have been spent up to the time of surrender and the amount actually spent shall be paid to the Government (Article 6). With respect to development leases, the right is given to Phillips to surrender its rights and interests in any such leases upon giving to Government at least one year's notice (Article 46). Somewhat similar provisions are found in the U.A.R.'s agreements with Pan American made in 1963 and 1964.

SECTION 2. ARBITRATION

In most oil concessions a provision exists for the settlement of disputes by means of arbitration. The arbitral provisions in oil concessions will be considered by the writer in a separate publication.[1a]

SECTION 3. AREA OF CONCESSION

The previous practice of conceding the whole territory of the State or the major part of such territory as the area of an oil concession has now been discontinued. The only recent exception is found in Jordan's concession to Mecom (1964). This concession covered the whole territory of Jordan.

[1a] See *The Law of Oil Concessions in the Middle East and North Africa* by the author.

The present practice is for the State to parcel out its territory into several areas which are then offered for oil exploitation under different concessions, or search permits, where applicable. This is now the practice followed in Libya, Iran, Algeria, the U.A.R., Tunisia and Morocco.

Countries which have enacted petroleum laws have limited by statute the areas that can be granted for oil concessions. The Libyan Petroleum Law, for example, divides the country into four zones (Article 3) and limits the number and the geographical area of the concessions that may be held at one time by any person (Article 9). The Iranian Petroleum Act prescribes that NIOC may divide the territory of the country, including the continental shelf but excluding the area covered by the agreement with the Consortium, into districts each of which shall consist of not more than 80,000 square kilometres and may invite offers to enter into agreements in relation thereto (Article 5). The Act further provides that at least one-third of the total exploitable area, including the continental shelf, shall be conserved at all times as a national reserve. The same limitations as to area are found in the oil legislations of Algeria and Morocco.

SECTION 4. ASSIGNMENT

Almost all concessions give to the concessionaire the right, subject to certain conditions, to assign the concession. The general rule is that no assignment or sale of the concessionaire's rights, powers or interests under the concession is permissible without first obtaining the permission of the conceding State or authority. An exception is usually made in the case of an assignment in favour of an operating company formed by the concessionaire for the purpose of carrying out the concessionaire's rights and obligations. Some concessions, however, have embodied additional conditions concerning assignment. Reference will be made here only to concessions which have departed from the usual pattern in this respect.

An innovation in the matter of assignment was introduced in 1948 by Aminoil's agreement with Kuwait. The agreement gave the Government an option to acquire the rights and interest proposed to be sold by the company. The agreement stated that if the company desires to sell its rights, powers or interest under the agreement it shall first obtain the written permission of the Sheikh. Such a transfer can only be made to purchasers registered in the U.S.A. or within the British Empire. It was agreed that the Sheikh shall have the option to acquire at the same price and terms specified in any proposed transfer or sale the rights and interest being offered by the company (Article 14).

Getty's agreement contained stringent conditions with respect to assignment. Article 15 provided that the company shall not assign the concession except with the written approval of the Government provided that if the company shall agree to pay to the Government 25% of the net capital gain, if any, from the sale of such concession and shall propose to make such sale to an American or Western European corporation of good repute having net assets of not less than U.S. $30,000,000 the approval of the Government shall not be unreasonably withheld or delayed. The agreement further provided that in the event of any proposed sale of such concession the Government shall have the preferential right to repurchase the same upon the same terms upon which it is proposed to make such sale. In the event of any such repurchase by the Government the net capital gain or profit of the company on such sale and the share of the Government therein shall be computed on the same basis as in the case of a sale to any other party so that the Government will receive a discount equal to the amount of such share. However, the company was authorized within one year to assign the agreement and concession to an operating corporation to be formed by it and such operating corporation would stand in the place and stead of the company.

The Consortium's agreement with Iran distinguished between three cases of assignment: assignment to subsidiaries, assignment to third persons and assignment to affiliated companies. In the case of subsidiaries, it was agreed that any Consortium member may assign to one or more subsidiaries nominated by it to act as Trading company or companies a part or all of that member's rights and obligations pertaining to purchases and resales, Iran and NIOC consenting in advance to any such assignment, provided that no such assignment shall relieve any such Consortium member of its obligations under the agreement (Article 18). With respect to third persons, the agreement provided that every Consortium member shall have the right to assign to another person upon the condition that such person, if not already a party to the agreement, becomes a party to the agreement and assumes all the obligations of the Consortium member and provided also that no such assignment shall be effective until Iran has given its consent thereto. In the case of an assignment to an affiliated company of the Consortium member, no such consent shall be required provided that such assignment shall not relieve such Consortium member from its obligations under the agreement (Article 39).

Iran's agreement with Pan American authorized Pan American to assign its rights and obligations to any company that it controls or to any company that controls Pan American. Any other assignment requires the prior written approval of NIOC. An identical provision was embodied in Sapphire's agreement. Somewhat similar provisions were included in Iran's recent Offshore agreements.

Kuwait's agreement with Arabian Oil Company embodied the general rule that the company may not without written consent assign the agreement. It further provided: (a) that the Sheikh shall have the right to acquire 10% of the issued share capital of the assignee at par or at the issue price, whichever shall be the lesser; and (b) that the Sheikh shall have the option to acquire, at the same price and terms specified in any proposed assignment, the rights and interest offered by the company.

The U.A.R.'s agreements with Phillips and Pan American stated that the grantees may not assign any of their rights, privileges, duties or obligations without the written consent of the Government. However, they shall be free to assign to an affiliated company provided that the assignee shall be as qualified as the assignor with respect to its technical and financial competence and is acceptable to the Government.

SECTION 5. CONTRACTORS

Concessions sometimes contain provisions relating to the use of contractors.

IPC's convention stated that the company shall have the right to place contracts for drilling, pipe-laying and other works within Iraq.

Aminoil's agreement stated that in its use of harbours the company shall use the services of local contracting concerns to such extent as is possible.

Getty's agreement stipulated that the company shall have the right to delegate to third parties the execution of operations covered by the agreement provided that the approval of the Government, which approval shall not be unreasonably withheld or delayed, shall be obtained to the employment of contractors not otherwise entitled to carry on business in Saudi Arabia and provided that Saudi Arabian contractors be given preference under equal conditions and circumstances. In the event of such delegation, such third parties shall enjoy all the rights and privileges guaranteed to the company by the agreement insofar as such rights and privileges shall pertain to operations of the character carried on by them in connection with the concession.

The Iranian Petroleum Act permits the use of foreign contractors only on the basis of reciprocity. The Act states that no operator may entrust his operations to a contractor except after having obtained the agreement of NIOC. Authority with respect to the use of foreign contractors will be granted only in cases where, under the current laws and economic regime of the foreign country concerned, Iranian persons would be permitted in general to engage in economic activities similar to those envisaged by the Act in the territory of such foreign country. Iran's oil agreements provide that the companies may engage such contractors fulfilling the requirements of the Petroleum Act for the purpose of carrying out any of the operations authorized under the agreement and NIOC grants its consent in advance to the use of such contractors.

Kuwait's agreement with Shell required the company to give preference to the employment of Kuwaiti contractors where the works to be carried out by them are within their abilities and their terms are reasonably competitive. It was further stipulated that in its use of Kuwaiti harbours, the company shall use the services of local concerns to such extent as is possible.

The U.A.R.'s agreements with Phillips and Pan American required the grantees, their operators and contractors to give priority to local contractors as long as their prices and performance are comparable with international prices and performance. These agreements also provided that contractors and subcontractors shall be subject to the provisions of the agreement and shall be bound by all regulations which are duly issued by the Government from time to time.

Saudi Arabia's agreement with Auxirap has required the company to give priority as far as possible to Saudi Arabian contractors, provided that the rates, terms and quality of work are the same as those obtainable in other countries.

SECTION 6. DRILLING AND EXPLORATION OBLIGATIONS

Early concessions were not exacting with respect to drilling or exploration. In fact, some concessions did not even impose any specific obligation in this respect. Recent oil concession agreements, however, impose drilling and exploration obligations. Such obligations assume various forms: either the number of wells to be drilled is fixed in advance or an obligation is imposed to maintain one or more rigs in operation or to drill to a certain aggregate depth or the obligation is translated into a fixed amount of guaranteed expenditure on exploration. We have already referred to the assumption by the concessionaire of exploration expenditure in discussing the financial conditions of concessions and we shall restrict ourselves here to a review of the other forms of exploration obligations.

IPC's agreement (1925) required the company within 32 months after the date of the convention to select 24 rectangular plots of an area of 8 square miles each and, within three years after the date of the convention, to start drilling operations therein, working continuously with a minimum of 6 rigs. After three years from the date of the convention the drilling obligation was imposed in terms of drilling depth (Article 5).

Aramco's agreement (1933) required the company to commence exploration work within three months and drilling operations as soon as a suitable structure was found. Once commenced, these operations were to continue diligently until oil was found in commercial quantities or the contract was terminated. After the date of discovery of oil in commercial quantities the company was required to continue drilling operations by using at least two strings of tools (Article 10).

KOC's agreement required the company to drill to a total aggregate depth of 4,000 feet within the four years following the date of the agreement, to a total aggregate depth of 12,000 feet within 10 years and to a total aggregate depth of 30,000 feet within 20 years from the date of the agreement. The drilling was to be carried out in such places as the company may decide. Kuwait's agreement with Aminoil imposed a drilling obligation also measured by total aggregate depth ranging from 4,000 feet within four years from the date of the agreement to 56,000 feet within 20 years (Article 2).

Getty's agreement required the concessionaire to commence exploratory operations within 9 months and to commence drilling operations within one year to a total aggregate depth of 6,000 feet to be increased to 16,000 feet before the end of three years.

Kuwait's agreement with Shell required the company, within 30 months from the effective date, to spud in a test well. Thereafter, the company shall proceed with the drilling of a test well or wells to an aggregate depth of not less than 20,000 feet, unless oil is discovered in commercial quantities before reaching that aggregate depth. Similarly, the agreement betwen the Ruler of Ras Al Khaima and Kuamco Oil imposed an obligation on the company to drill to an aggregate depth of 20,000 feet (Article 3).

The U.A.R.'s practice with regard to the concessionaire's drilling obligations is somewhat similar to that followed by Iran in requiring a monetary amount to be spent on exploration. The drilling obligation is translated into guaranteed exploration expenditures undertaken by the concessionaire. The U.A.R.'s agreement with Phillips, in addition to providing for a guaranteed minimum expenditure, also stipulated that, as part of the concessionaire's obligation in this respect, Phillips shall commence the drilling of an exploration well before two years from the date of the agreement and before the expiration of the fourth year Phillips shall commence the drilling of three other wells. The obligation on the concessionaire to drill four wells in accordance with a prescribed timetable is also laid down in the U.A.R.'s agreements with Pan American.

SECTION 7. DURATION OF CONCESSION

We have seen how in early days oil concessions were granted for long periods.[2] However, since mid-century concessions are granted for shorter terms. Exceptionally, the terms of the concession granted by Qatar to Shell Overseas Exploration Company in 1952 was for 75 years. Since that date no concessions were granted for such long

---

[2] Section 1 of Chapter I.

periods and the average term of concessions now varies between 25 and 50 years, usually with an option for one or more short term extensions.

The Libyan Petroleum Law prescribes that the period of concessions shall not exceed 50 years with the possibility of renewal for any period such that the total of the two periods does not exceed 60 years (Article 9).

The Egyptian Law of Mines and Quarries of 1953, as amended in 1956, limits the duration of mineral concessions to an original period of 30 years, with an option for two further extensions of 15 years each. Thus, the agreement between the U.A.R. and Phillips is for 30 years with a right for its extension to an additional period of 15 years. A similar term is provided in the U.A.R.'s agreements with Pan American.

In the past, the period of the concession began from the date of signature or the date of the coming into force of the concession. In a number of recent cases the period of the concession begins effectively to run from the date of discovery of oil. Such is the practice in Iran. The Iranian Petroleum Act states in Article 7 that the original period of the oil agreement may not exceed 25 years from the date of commercial production, but the period may be renewed for no more than three terms of 5 years each. However, the second and third renewals are subject to such more favourable conditions as are in effect at the time of such renewals. The recent Iranian Offshore agreements (1965) make the term of the agreements run from the date of commencement of commercial production which is defined as the exportation of 100,000 cubic metres of petroleum.

The agreement between Saudi Arabia and Japan Petroleum Trading Company stipulated a term of 40 years commencing from the date of discovery of oil in commercial quantities. The agreement made between Kuwait and Arabian Oil Company was for a period of 44½ years from the date of signature of the agreement. Saudi Arabia's agreement with Auxirap (1965) stipulated the grant of a lease for a term of 30 years upon the discovery of oil in commercial quantities.

Shell's concession from Kuwait was made for a period of 45 years from the date of signature.

The agreement between the Ruler of Ras Al Khaima and Kuamco Oil has a life of 40 years.

Mecom's recent agreement with Jordan was concluded for a period of 40 years.

The Sahara Petroleum Code fixed the period of concession at 50 years (Article 28). Inasmuch as concessions are granted under this Code only after the discovery of oil, it follows that the exploration period is not taken into account in determining the life of the concession.

SECTION 8. EMPLOYMENT OF NATIONALS

The obligation of the concessionaire to employ national labour and skill has become a common condition of oil concessions. In recent concessions, such obligation has been translated into a percentage of total employment.

Aramco's concession provided that the enterprise shall be directed and supervised by Americans who shall employ Saudi Arab nationals as far as practicable.

The concessions granted under the Libyan Petroleum Law required that the number of Libyan subjects employed by the concessionaire after 10 years shall be at least 75% of total employment by the concessionaire in Libya provided that the requisite number having adequate skill and ability is available.

The Iranian agreements generally require the taking of steps for the gradual and progressive reduction of foreign personnel. The Consortium's agreement required the Operating Companies to minimize the employment of foreign personnel by ensuring so far as reasonably practicable that foreign personnel are engaged to occupy positions for which the Operating Companies do not find available Iranians of the requisite qualifications and experience. The agreement further required that the Operating Companies shall prepare plans and programs for industrial and technical training and education with a view to training Iranians to replace foreign personnel as soon as reasonably practicable. AGIP's agreement provided that the use of foreign staff shall be within reasonable limits. Such foreign staff shall be recruited only to fill positions for which Iranian nationals having the required qualifications and experience cannot be found. In addition, the concessionaire undertook to draw up a program for the technical and industrial training of Iranian personnel.

Subsequent agreements made by Iran with Pan American and Sapphire have gone further and have fixed a deadline for the reduction of foreign personnel. They have provided that upon the expiry of ten years from the date of the agreement the number of foreign nationals employed shall not exceed 2% of the total personnel while the top executive positions occupied by non-Iranians shall not exceed 49% of the total of executive positions available. Identical provisions limiting the employment of foreign personnel were included in Iran's Offshore agreements of January 16, 1965.

The Kuwait-Shell agreement required the company to train and employ subjects of the Emir as far as practicable for all works in the management and operations of its activities for which they are suited. As far as practicable 70% of its labour and employees in Kuwait shall be subjects of the Emir and 90% of its unskilled labour shall be subjects of the Emir or subjects of neighbouring countries.

The agreement between the U.A.R. and Phillips provided that the special residence and work permits and alien work permits required by law shall be granted to expatriate administrative and technical personnel of the concessionaire. But the concessionaire undertook, to the extent that qualified persons are available, to replace gradually the expatriate staff by nationals of the U.A.R. A similar provision was included in the agreements made between the U.A.R. and Pan American.

Saudi Arabia's agreement with Auxirap required that 75% of the company's employees in Saudi Arabia shall be Saudis and 30% of its employees outside Saudi Arabia shall also be Saudis, if available.

SECTION 9. FORCE MAJEURE

Almost all oil agreements include a provision with respect to *force majeure* and apply the general legal rule that failure due to *force majeure* shall not be treated as a breach of contract. In many cases also, the occurrence of *force majeure* gives a right to an extension of the term of the concession or of the time required to perform an obligation corresponding to the delay occasioned by such event. Variations exist between concessions in regard to the definition and effects of *force majeure*.

IPC's agreement with Iraq stated that no failure or omission on

the part of the company to carry out or perform any of the stipulations, covenants or conditions of the convention shall give the Government any claim against the company or be deemed a breach of the
convention insofar as the same arises from *force majeure*. The convention further provided that, if through *force majeure* the fulfilment
by the company of any of the conditions of the convention be delayed,
the period of such delay shall be added to the periods fixed by the
convention, provided always that no such addition shall be made
unless the production or export of petroleum by the company shall be
totally suspended for not less than 60 consecutive days through *force
majeure* occurring within Iraq (Article 39).

Aramco's concession provided in Article 27 that no failure or
omission on the part of the company to carry out or to perform any
of the terms or conditions of the contract shall give the Government
any claim against the company or be deemed a breach of the contract
insofar as such failure or omission may arise from *force majeure*. If
through *force majeure* the fulfilment of any term or condition of the
contract should be delayed, the period of the delay, together with such
period as may be required for the restoration of any damage done
during such delay, shall be added to the terms or periods fixed in
the contract.

KOC's agreement stated in Article 16 that failure on the part of
the company to fulfil any condition of the agreement shall not be
deemed a breach of the agreement insofar as such failure arises from
force majeure and if through *force majeure* the fulfilment by the
company of any condition of the agreement be delayed, the period of
such delay shall be added to the periods fixed by the agreement.

Getty's agreement contained the usual clause providing that failure to perform an obligation under the agreement shall not constitute
a default insofar as such failure arises from *force majeure* and to the
extent of any delay caused thereby the period of such delay shall be
added to the period fixed by the agreement for such performance.
Force majeure is defined by Article 44 to include "Act of God, war,
insurrection, riot, civil commotion, strike, tide, storm, tidal wave,
flood, lightning, explosion, fire, earthquake, interruption of facilities
for transportation or communication, interference with the exercise
of the rights of either party by any third party and any other event
which may not reasonably be prevented or controlled". The same

enumeration of *force majeure* causes—with the omission of "Act of God," an untranslatable term of art—occurs in Saudi Arabia's agreements with Japan Petroleum Trading Company and Auxirap.

The Libyan Petroleum Law, as amended in 1961, stated that in the event of *force majeure* the rights and obligations of the parties shall be those specified in the concession agreement. The form of the concession agreement prescribed by the Law provides that failure by the company to carry out any of the provisions of its concession shall not be deemed a breach if it be shown that the failure has arisen from *force majeure* or any unforeseen circumstances beyond the control of the company. If by reason of *force majeure* the fulfilment by the company of any of the terms and conditions of its concession or the enjoyment of its rights under the concession is delayed, the period of such delay shall be added to the period fixed for such fulfilment or enjoyment.

AGIP's agreement with Iran enumerated in Article 37 certain events which shall excuse performance. The same Article further provided that events other than those listed shall be deemed to be beyond the control of the parties when so understood by international law. This provision is in line with the Iranian Petroleum Act which states in Article 13 that "*force majeure* means occurrences that are recognized as such by the principles of international law". The same rules concerning *force majeure* are found in Iran's agreements with Pan American and Sapphire.

Iran's recent Offshore agreements (1965) lay down specifically the effects flowing from *force majeure*. They state in Article 36 that where any *force majeure* occurrence beyond the reasonable control of the second party (i.e., NIOC's partner in the joint venture) or the jointly owned operating company renders impossible or hinders or delays the performance of any obligation or the exercise of any right under the agreement, then:

(a) this failure or omission of the second party or the operating company to perform such obligation shall not be treated as a failure or omission to comply with the agreement;

(b) the period whereby such performance or such exercise is delayed shall be added to any relevant periods fixed by the agreement; and

(c) if the duration of such occurrence is not less than one

year, the agreement shall automatically be extended for a period equal to the duration of such occurrence, without prejudice to any right to further extensions under the agreement.

It is further provided that such provisions shall not prevent the second party from referring to arbitration the question of whether or not the agreement should be dissolved by total impossibility of performance.

One recent agreement has somewhat deviated from the accepted rules governing the effect of *force majeure*. Kuwait's agreement with Arabian Oil Company embodied the usual rule that failure on the part of the company to fulfil any of its obligations shall not be deemed a breach of the agreement insofar as such failure arises from *force majeure*. However, in the event of the company failing to make any royalty or other payment, such failure having arisen from *force majeure*, the company shall, if so required by the Sheikh, discontinue its operations until the cause of such failure shall have been removed. If such cause shall not have been removed for a period of twelve months, the Sheikh shall have the right to terminate the agreement (Article 30). A similar power was reserved for the Emir to request the discontinuance of operations upon the failure of the company for six months to make any royalty or other payment—but not to terminate the agreement—in Article 26 of Kuwait's agreement with Shell.

The U.A.R.'s agreement with Phillips also contained the usual clause about *force majeure* and the provision that non-performance or delay in performance by Phillips is excused if and to the extent that such non-performance or delay is caused by *force majeure*. The agreement, however, embodied a novel provision to the extent that in defining *force majeure* it included within the definition "any order, regulation or direction of the Government of the U.A.R. or the Government of the other contracting party, whether promulgated in the form of a law or otherwise". It provided, however, that the Government shall incur no responsibility whatsoever to Phillips for any damages, restrictions or loss arising in consequence of such case of *force majeure*, except a *force majeure* caused by the order, regulation or direction of the Government of the U.A.R. (Article 47). The subsequent agreements made with Pan American have included a similar provision.

The situation in which *force majeure* results in total impossibility of performance will be discussed in Section 21, *post*.

SECTION 10. LAW APPLICABLE TO CONCESSION

In some cases the law applicable to the oil concession is specifically stated either in a statute or in the agreement. Contractual stipulations in oil concessions regarding the applicable law will not be examined here inasmuch as they will receive consideration in a separate study.[2a]

SECTION 11. MOST FAVOURED COMPANY CLAUSE

The "most favoured company clause" is a provision of a new kind which we find in two classes of agreements. The object of the provision is different in each case.

This provision is found first in the agreements concluded early in 1965 between oil companies and certain OPEC countries with regard to the expensing of royalties. Its purpose is to preserve the competitive position of companies operating within the same country. Reduced to the simplest language possible under the circumstances, the basic idea underlying this type of clause is to ensure that an oil company shall not be required in any one year to make to the Government total payments which when aggregated would be greater than the aggregate amounts that would be payable by such company if there were applicable to it in respect of such year the most favourable arrangements applicable to any other enterprise engaged in producing crude oil in the same country. This principle, however, is subject to two reservations:

(1) In order that a fair comparison can be made between the amounts paid and amounts otherwise payable, the latter shall be equitably adjusted for the purposes of such comparison. In making such equitable adjustment the parties shall have due regard to the basic differences between the provisions of the respective agreements, arrangements and circumstances relating to the activities or operations of the company and those relating to the activities or operations of the other enterprise, including

---

[2a] See *The Law of Oil Concessions in the Middle East and North Africa* by the author.

but not limited to any burdens directly or indirectly relating to or arising out of such activities or operations;

(2) The aggregate amounts payable in respect of any year by the company shall not as a result of the application of the preceding provisions be less than the aggregate of the payments which the company would have been obliged to make to the Government in respect of such year calculated in accordance with the arrangements prevailing between the parties immediately prior to the date of the new agreement.

A most favoured company clause of another kind is that found in the Iranian Offshore agreements (1965). It will be recalled that such agreements envisage that the parties shall not be subject to rates of income tax which are less favourable than those applicable to other companies engaged in similar operations which together produce more than 50% of Iranian crude oil.

Finally, a most favourable treatment provision figures in the NIOC-AGIP agreement (1957) with respect to payments for services. Article 17 of the agreement states that SIRIP shall be liable to pay for any service rendered (water and electricity supplies, pilots' services in harbours, sewage and health services) but SIRIP shall enjoy the most favourable treatment granted to other users.

SECTION 12. MOST FAVOURED NATION CLAUSE

The nearest approach to a most favoured nation clause in oil concession agreements was a provision included in an exchange of letters between Iraq and IPC in 1951. By a letter dated September 28, 1951, Iraq asked the IPC group of companies to take note that if, in the future, arrangements are made between the Governments of Persia, Saudi Arabia or Kuwait and any other party in regard to the development of oil fields and the production of crude oil, which result in any such Government receiving a higher average revenue per ton than Iraq, the Government will consider itself entitled to receive from the companies an average revenue per ton not less than that received by any such Government. By their reply bearing the same date, the companies assured the Government that, in the circumstances envisaged in the Government's letter, they would be willing to consider and discuss the position with the Government of Iraq.

A most favoured nation clause, limited both as to time and space, was included in the concession granted by the Sultan of Muscat and Oman on January 17, 1953 to Philpryor Corporation.[3] The concession provided as follows:

"With respect to any matters which will not be covered by this concession, the company agrees that when and if oil is discovered and recovered in commercial quantities for regular export this concession shall be revised so that its terms shall not be less favourable than the terms now (at the signing of this concession) in force in the oil concessions of Kuwait and Saudi Arabia."

The Iranian Petroleum Act takes into account the existence of more favourable terms in other agreements at the time of the second and third renewals of an oil agreement. Article 7 of the Act provides that the original term of 25 years contemplated for oil agreements may be renewed for three terms of 5 years each. The first renewal will be effected in accordance with the original terms, but in respect of the two further renewals, the operator seeking the renewal must accept the conditions, privileges and circumstances in effect at the time of such renewal. In implementation of this principle the agreement made between NIOC and Pan American embodied a provision stating that if at the time when the concessionaire requests the second and third renewals other foreign oil companies—associated with NIOC in view of a similar activity and having already achieved production results equal or superior to those achieved by the "joint structure" existing between NIOC and Pan American—shall have concluded agreements containing conditions which are on the whole more favourable to Iran than those contained in the agreement, all such conditions of the said agreements shall apply to the renewals requested by Pan American. A similar clause is found in the agreement made between NIOC and Sapphire and in Article 33 of the Iranian Offshore agreements of January 16, 1965.

Although, strictly speaking, not amounting to a most favoured nation clause, a provision requiring "review of the situation" or "consultation between the parties" in the event that more favourable concession agreements are concluded by the concessionaire or sometimes by neighbouring countries has been included in some oil agreements. Thus, Bapco undertook in 1952 that if States other than Bahrain bordering the Arabian Gulf in which oil was then produced should receive substantially better terms than the Ruler of Bahrain,

---

[3] This concession was subsequently assigned to Cities Service Company.

the company would be willing "to review the situation". Similarly, the Consortium agreed in 1954 with Iran that if during the term of the agreement two or more of the initial Consortium members reach a new arrangement with any other country bordering on the Arabian Gulf whereby that country's percentage share of profit is higher than the share of Iran in the profits from operations under the agreement, then Iran will consult with the Consortium members with a view to determining whether it would be equitable that an appropriate modification of the agreement should be made.

The agreement between Kuwait and Arabian Oil Company (1958) stated in Article 38 that if in the future arrangements are made between the Governments of other Middle Eastern countries and any other party which result in any such Government receiving a higher proportion of the profits of development of oil fields, production and marketing than that specified in the agreement, the company will be willing to review and discuss the situation with the Sheikh in the light of the new terms and all other relevant facts and circumstances.

The Kuwait-Shell agreement (1961) similarly provided in Article 27 that, if as a result of changes in the terms of concessions in existence at the time of the agreement or as a result of the terms of concessions granted thereafter, an increase in benefits to Governments in the Middle East should come generally to be received by them, the company will consult with the Emir, whether in the light of all relevant circumstances, including the conditions in which operations are carried out and taking into account all payments made, any alteration to the terms of the agreement would be equitable to the parties.

A similarly worded condition was inserted in the supplemental agreement concluded between Kuwait and Aminoil in 1961 and in the agreement made between the Ruler of Ras Al Khaima and Kuamco Oil in 1962.

SECTION 13. NO UNILATERAL ABROGATION OR MODIFICATION OF THE CONCESSION

A large number of oil agreements embody provisions which stipulate that the Government shall not modify or abrogate the concession and that no alteration shall be made therein except by mutual consent of the parties.

One may perhaps doubt whether such provisions add anything to the legal force and effect of agreements. Under the ordinary rules of law, contracts can be altered or modified only by mutual consent of the parties. A possible construction of such provisions is that they may amount to a negation of the administrative character of such contracts.[4]

The earliest of such provisions is found in Article 21 of AIOC's convention with Iran (1933). The agreement stated that the concession shall not be annulled by the Government and its term shall not be altered either by general or special legislation in the future or by administrative measures or any other act whatever of the executive authorities. It is ironical to remark that this concession was in fact annulled in 1951 in the very mode proscribed by the agreement itself.

Article 17 of KOC's agreement provided that the Sheikh shall not by general or special legislation or by administrative measures or by any other act whatever annul the agreement except in the specific case wherein the Sheikh has the right to terminate the agreement for breach by the company of certain of its obligations. The agreement further provided that no alteration shall be made in its terms by either party except in the event of the two parties jointly agreeing that it is desirable in their interests to make certain alterations or additions to the agreement. An identical provision was included in Article 17 of Aminoil's agreement.

The Consortium's agreement provided in Article 41 that no general or special legislative or administrative measures or any other act whatsoever of, or emanating from, Iran or any governmental authority in Iran, whether central or local, shall annul the agreement, amend or modify its provisions or prevent or hinder the due and effective performance of its terms. Such annulment, amendment or modification shall not take place except by agreement of the parties. A similar provision was embodied in Iran's agreements with Pan American and Sapphire and in Iran's Offshore agreements (1965).

Saudi Arabia's agreement with Japan Petroleum Trading Company stated that no changes in the clauses of the agreement and obligations of either party shall be made except by mutual agreement between the Government and the company. An identical provision occurs in Saudi Arabia's agreement with Auxirap.

---

[4] Dr. Mann doubts the legal validity of such provisions: F. A. Mann, State Contracts and State Responsibility, *AJIL* (1960), pp. 587–588.

Kuwait's agreement with Arabian Oil Company stated that the Sheikh shall not by general or special legislation or by administrative measures or by any other act annul the agreement except as therein provided. No alteration shall be made in its terms except by joint agreement of the parties. An identically worded provision is found in Kuwait's agreement with Shell.

The agreements made by the U.A.R. with Phillips and Pan American have provided that they can only be amended by agreement between the contracting parties.

The Libyan concessions embody a standard condition stating that the contractual rights expressly created by the concession shall not be altered except by the mutual consent of the parties.

SECTION 14. OFFICIAL TEXT

Concession agreements in the Middle East are usually written in two languages. It is therefore necessary to provide which of the two texts prevails or whether both have equal validity.

In the past, the rule was to provide that in case of divergence between the two texts, the foreign version shall prevail. In recent years the tendency has been to recognize the validity of the national language or to attribute equal weight to both languages.

The earliest oil concession in the Middle East (1901) was written in the French language and translated into Persian. It provided that in the event of there being any dispute with respect to its meaning, the French text alone shall prevail.

IPC's convention (1925) stated that in the event of any discrepancy between the meanings of the English and Arabic versions, the English version shall prevail. IPC's agreement of 1952 which amended the original convention stated that it has been drawn up in the Arabic and English languages, both texts being regarded as authoritative, but in the event of any discrepancy between the meanings of the English and Arabic texts, the English text shall prevail.

Aramco's concession provided that the contract has been drawn up in English and Arabic but inasmuch as most of the obligations thereunder are imposed upon the company and inasmuch as the interpretation of the English text, especially as regards technical obligations and requirements relating to the oil industry, has been fairly well established through long practice and experience in contracts such as the present one, it is agreed that while both texts shall have equal validity, nevertheless in case of any divergence of interpretation as to the Company's obligations under the agreement, the English text shall prevail.

KOC's agreement stated that if there should be any disagreement as to the meaning or interpretation of any clause in the agreement, the English text shall prevail. An identical provision occurred in Aminoil's agreement with Kuwait.

Getty's agreement introduced for the first time the concept of equal weight of the Arabic and English texts of the agreement. It stated that the agreement shall be signed in quadruplicate, two of such signed originals being in the Arabic language and two in the English language. Each of the parties shall retain one signed original in Arabic and one signed original in English. All of such signed originals shall be entitled to equal weight.

Saudi Arabia's agreement with Japan Petroleum Trading Company contained a somewhat similar provision and stated that all of the signed originals in Arabic and English shall be regarded as authoritative and shall be entitled to equal weight. The same provision occurs in Saudi Arabia's agreement with Auxirap.

The Consortium's agreement provided that the Persian and the English texts of the agreement are both valid. In case of dispute which is referred to arbitration, both texts shall be laid before the arbitration board or the sole arbitrator (as the case may be). The arbitration board or the arbitrator shall interpret the intention of the parties from both texts. If there is any divergence between the texts as to the rights and duties of the parties, the English text shall prevail.

AGIP's agreement with Iran mentioned that it was drafted in French, Persian and Italian and that the French draft shall be the official text but that, in case of recourse to arbitration, the Persian and Italian drafts may be submitted to the arbitrators to serve as auxiliary means of interpretation.

Iran's agreement with Pan American stated that the Persian and English texts of the agreement are both valid and, in case of a dispute which is referred to arbitration, the two texts shall be laid before the arbitrators who shall interpret the intention of the parties from both texts. If there is any divergence between the texts as to the rights and duties of the parties, the English text shall prevail. The same provision occurred in Iran's agreement with Sapphire and in its Offshore agreements (1965).

Kuwait's agreement with Arabian Oil Company stated that the agreement is written in English and translated into Arabic. If there should be disagreement as to its meaning or interpretation, the English text shall prevail. An identical clause figures in Kuwait's agreement with Shell (1961).

The U.A.R.'s agreement with Phillips provided that the Arabic version of the agreement which has been translated from the English version shall be the official text, but in the event any dispute is submitted to arbitration both the English and Arabic versions shall be presented to the arbitrators for their consideration. In any dispute between Phillips and EGPC which is submitted to arbitration if there should occur a conflict in the meaning of a particular word, phrase or provision as expressed in the English version and in the Arabic translation, the former shall prevail. Pan American's agreements with the U.A.R. have provided that the Arabic version which has been translated from the English version shall be referred to in construing or interpreting the agreement provided, however, that in any dispute or arbitration between EGPC and Pan American the English version shall also be used to construe or interpret the agreement.

SECTION 15. PRODUCTION CONTROL

In the past, the concern of the producing countries was the expansion of oil production in order to maximize their benefits. For this reason, very few oil concessions have embodied provisions for control, curtailment or regulation of oil production—except to the extent that special powers were envisaged in times of national emergency. Two instances, however, exist where the producing country has reserved the power to curtail or regulate oil production.

The first instance is found in Getty's concession in the Neutral Zone. Article 42 of the agreement provided that the company shall conduct its drilling and production operations according to all reasonable requirements, consistent with good oil field practice, as may be imposed upon all other companies conducting oil operations within the Kingdom of Saudi Arabia, for the purpose of conserving the national wealth; provided that if by reason of any curtailment imposed upon production the royalty payable under the agreement in any year shall be less than the minimum royalty fixed by the same agreement, then such minimum royalty shall be correspondingly reduced.

In the second instance, the producing country reserved to itself a much larger power, not only to limit but also to increase the level of production. Article 26 of the Sahara Petroleum Code (1958) provided that the concession agreement will lay down the general rules applicable to all producers according to which the authorities may fix the lower and higher limits of production taking into account economic conditions.

Recently, the question of oil production control has come to the fore with OPEC's resolution passed on July 13, 1965. This resolution referred to the continuing erosion of prices and mentioned that one of the contributing factors to their deterioration was the unrestricted competitive use of the excess producing capacity. Accordingly, the resolution adopted as a transitory measure a production plan calling for rational increases in production from the OPEC area to meet estimated increases in world demand and proposed to submit a production programme to the Governments of member countries for approval.

SECTION 16. PRODUCTION OBLIGATION

Early concession agreements were usually silent on the volume of oil production. Towards mid-century, some producing countries began to insist upon a certain volume of production. Iraq was the first to take the lead in this respect. Its agreement with IPC (1952) embodied the company's undertaking that it will produce and dispose of a minimum quantity of 20¾ million tons of crude oil per annum. Production obligations were also the subject of agreement between Iraq and the Mosul and Basrah Oil Companies.

The Consortium's agreement embodied both a production obligation and a production guarantee. The production obligation covered the quantity required for internal consumption in Iran, the quantity, if any, taken as royalty oil and the quantity required by the Trading Companies as determined by them. The production guarantee provided that the crude oil exported or delivered to the refinery or delivered as royalty oil shall reach an aggregate of 35 million cubic metres within three years. Following the period in which the guaranteed quantity of 35 million cubic metres shall have been attained, it will be the policy of the Consortium members, assuming favourable operating and economic conditions in Iran, to adjust the quantity so attained in such manner as will reasonably reflect the supply and demand for Middle East crude oil.

The Iranian agreements with AGIP, Pan American and Sapphire did not impose any volume of production. They provided in general terms that the company shall use its best endeavours to raise its oil sales to the highest level and for this purpose to develop the yield of each deposit by using every means of production within the limits consistent with recent processes used in the petroleum industry. The Iranian Offshore agreements (1965) have provided that each party shall exercise its utmost efforts in order to ensure the sale of the maximum possible quantity of petroleum economically justified and that they shall agree on a procedure for offtake requirements and programmes.

Kuwait's agreement with Arabian Oil Company contained a general obligation to produce at the maximum efficient rate provided that a satisfactory market exists for the petroleum produced. A similar general obligation occurs in Saudi Arabia's agreement with Auxirap.

SECTION 17. REFINING

Early concessions either granted the concessionaire refining rights without any corresponding obligation on his part, or imposed a refining obligation limited to the needs of local consumption. For example, IPC's concession (1925) required the company to refine such petroleum, kerosene and fuel oil as may be required from time to time for local consumption. A somewhat similar provision is found in Aramco's concession. The agreement stated that after the discovery of oil in commercial quantities the company shall erect a plant for manufacturing sufficient gasoline and kerosene to meet the ordinary requirements of the Government.

Some recent concessions still grant refining rights without imposing any corresponding obligations, such as the Iranian agreements with AGIP and Pan American. The Libyan concessions belong to the same category. It is provided in Article 21 of the Libyan Petroleum

Law that the concession holder who discovers petroleum in Libya and who desires to refine it in the country shall have the right to construct, maintain and operate a refinery for this purpose in accordance with any legislation governing the refining of petroleum. The Law also states that should refineries be established in Libya the Petroleum Commission (now the Ministry of Petroleum Affairs) may require a concession holder to make available to such refineries *pro rata* with other concession holders sufficient quantities of crude oil to meet the domestic consumption requirements of Libya in respect of petroleum products.

The recent Iranian Offshore agreements do not include any rights or obligations with respect to refining and envisage that refineries can be constructed only in extension of the terms of the agreements (Article 10).

Some recent concessions have imposed refining obligations not limited to the satisfaction of internal requirements but designed to promote the development of a local refining industry. It should, however, be observed that in all such cases the refining obligation matures only after production has reached a substantial level. We find examples of such provisions in the following concessions. Aminoil's concession in the Neutral Zone stated that, if and when there is reached a daily production of 15,000 English tons, the company pledges itself to construct a modern and suitable oil refinery having a capacity of not less than 10% of the 15,000 tons daily production. The refinery shall be owned by a subsidiary of the concessionaire and the Sheikh shall receive 15% of its capital stock without any financial contribution on his part. Getty's concession also provided that when crude oil produced shall have averaged 75,000 U.S. barrels per day for a period of 90 days the company shall construct in the Neutral Zone a modern refinery having a minimum daily throughput capacity of 12,000 barrels of crude oil, unless the Government shall dispense with the requirement of the building of such refinery. Saudi Arabia's concession to Japan Petroleum Trading Company required the concessionaire to construct a refinery within two years after the crude oil produced from the concession area shall have averaged 30,000 barrels per day for a period of 90 days. The concession further stipulated that when production shall have averaged 75,000 barrels per day for a period of 90 days the concessionaire shall construct a refinery or refineries having a minimum daily throughput capacity of not less than 30% of the company's production. Kuwait's concession to Arabian Oil Company contained similar provisions as to the building of refineries as in the concession granted by Saudi Arabia to Japan Petroleum Trading Company. Shell's agreement with Kuwait provided that after a substantial daily rate of production of crude petroleum has been reached and adequate reserves have been discovered to maintain this rate of production for a substantial period, the company undertakes to discuss and decide with the Emir whether or not a suitable oil refinery or other plant for treatment of petroleum shall be constructed by the company in Kuwait. Among the factors to be taken into account in reaching a decision shall be (a) the desirability of increasing by the erection of such refinery or plant in the State of Kuwait the profit in which the Emir is to share from the company's operations and (b) the economics of refining or treating petroleum in Kuwait to the company.

Pan American's concession in Hadramaut imposed upon the company the obligation to construct a refinery sufficiently large to provide for the local requirements of petroleum products. Such refinery shall be constructed at such time as the Company shall have exported an average of 40,000 barrels of crude oil per day over a 90-day period.

Saudi Arabia's agreement with Auxirap stated that when the crude oil produced shall have averaged 100,000 barrels per day for a period of 90 days the company shall construct a refinery in Saudi Arabia having a minimum daily throughput capacity of not less than 30,000 barrels per day, unless such a capacity would result in a loss for the company, in which case the parties shall agree on the proper capacity to be followed.

SECTION 18. RELINQUISHMENT

The subject of relinquishment has been discussed in Section 2B of Chapter I.

SECTION 19. REMEDIES FOR BREACH

Concessions have always provided for the consequences of, and remedies for, breach of the agreement by the parties. More often, however, agreements are concerned with a breach by the concessionaire.

A noticeable evolution has occurred with respect to the definition of the remedies for a breach committed by the concessionaire. The predominant rule in the past was to consider the payment of damages as the ordinary remedy for breach, except where the agreement stipulated a right to terminate the agreement on account of such breach. It was not uncommon to specify in the agreement certain basic obligations which, if violated by the concessionaire, would give the Government the right to cancel or terminate the agreement. An analysis of recent oil agreements reveals a diversity of remedies available in case of breach by the concessionaire of his obligations. These remedies could be:

(1) Damages;

(2) Cancellation of the agreement, either by decision of an arbitration tribunal or by a unilateral decision of the conceding State after notice to the concessionaire. In some cases, the cancellation of the concession can take place only as a result of certain defined violations or if the arbitrators so decide;

(3) Coercive measures by the conceding State.

We shall now review the provisions of the principal concessions with respect to these remedies.

D'Arcy's concession stated that if the concessionaire shall not have established the first of the companies for the working of the concession within two years, the concession shall become null and void.

IPC's original concession (1925) stated in Article 37 that except as otherwise provided in Articles 4 (relating to the geographical survey to be performed by the concessionaire), 5 (relating to the concessionaire's drilling obligations), 13 (non-payment of royalties after the expiration of a specified period) and 36 (concerning the deposit of securities as guarantee for the expenditure of a specified amount on operations), the penalty for any breach of the convention shall be damages which shall be fixed by agreement or arbitration. Iraq's amended convention with IPC (1952) stipulated that the Government shall have the right to terminate the amended convention if payments due to the Government were not paid within a prescribed time.

AIOC's convention (1933) provided in Article 26 that the con-

cession can come to an end before its due date only in the case of
surrender by the company of the concession or in the case that the
arbitration court should declare the concession annulled as a consequence of the company's default in the performance of the agreement.
The following cases only shall be regarded as default in this sense:

(i) If any sum awarded to Persia by the arbitration court
has not been paid within one month of the date of the award;

(ii) In case of liquidation of the company.

In any other cases of breach of the agreement by one party or the
other, the arbitration court shall establish the responsibilities and
determine their consequences.

Kuwait's agreement with KOC gave the Sheikh the right to
terminate the agreement for certain specified breaches committed by
the company. On such termination, all the property of the company
within Kuwait became the property of the Sheikh. An identical provision as to termination was embodied in Kuwait's agreement with
Aminoil.

Aramco's concession (1933) enumerated in Article 30 certain
obligations, the breach of which entitled the Government to give
notice to the company to remedy such breach and in the event of
failure to remedy the breach, the Government could terminate the
contract. However, except as otherwise provided, the penalty for the
breach by the company of any of its obligations shall be damages to
be determined by agreement or arbitration.

Getty's agreement (1949) provided that if either party is of the
opinion that the other party is in default in its obligations it shall
give notice to the other party to that effect and in such event the
recipient of the notice may have the issue determined by arbitration. If the recipient fails to apply for arbitration then such party
shall be deemed to be in default and shall remedy such default within
90 days after receipt of the notice. If the defaulting party is the company and fails to remedy the default or fails to comply with the
decision of the board of arbitration in this respect, the Government
may terminate the agreement (Article 43).

The Consortium's agreement with Iran laid down in detail the
procedure to be followed in the case of a breach by either party. It
stated in Article 42 that if in the opinion of any party to the agreement any other party is in default in the performance of any obligation

thereunder, the first party shall first give the other party written notice specifying the respects in which a default is believed to exist and calling upon such other party to remedy the default. Unless the matter is disposed of by agreement within 30 days after the receipt of such notice or such longer period as may be agreed to by the parties, then the complaint may be referred to a Conciliation Committee under the provisions of the agreement. Any complaint which either party does not wish to refer to a Conciliation Committee, or which is not determined by a binding ruling, i.e., a unanimous ruling of the said Committee, may be submitted to arbitration. The Consortium's agreement also provided in Article 41 that, unless the parties otherwise agree, the agreement shall not be terminated or dissolved prior to the expiration of its term except by a decision made by an arbitration board or sole arbitrator that it has been terminated by breach or dissolved by total impossibility of performance. Other oil agreements made by Iran apply substantially the same provisions with respect to breach as those embodied in the Consortium's agreement.

In Libya, the Petroleum Law stated that a permit or concession granted under the Law may be revoked only in the circumstances and in the manner set out in the permit or concession. The standard form of the Libyan concession agreement provides that the Commission (now the Ministry of Petroleum Affairs) may revoke the concession if the company fails to commence operations or meet its expenditure obligations within the time prescribed, or if any surface rents or royalties are in arrears for six months, or if the company goes into liquidation, or if the company fails in its relinquishment obligations, or assigns its concession without the consent of the Commission, or fails to pay within 90 days of the date fixed in the award any sum awarded against the company in arbitration proceedings. Whenever the company disputes the revocation and requests arbitration, the revocation shall only become effective subject to and in accordance with the result of the arbitration (Clause 27).

Saudi Arabia's agreement with Japan Petroleum Trading Company stated that the penalty for breach by the company of any of its obligations under the agreement for which no provision is made in the agreement or in the Income Tax Law shall be damages to be determined by agreement or arbitration. However, the agreement reserved the company's right to demand that the question as to whether or not the company has committed a breach be submitted to arbitration (Article 51).

The U.A.R.'s practice in this matter is different. Its agreements with Phillips and Pan American have provided that if the Government deems that a cause exists to cancel the agreement, the Government shall give to the other party 90 days written notice to remedy and remove such cause. If on expiration of the period of the notice such cause has not been remedied and removed, the agreement may be cancelled forthwith by order or decree.

The last remedy for breach of the agreement by the concessionaire is a recent development: it is neither damages nor cancellation, but the taking by the Government of certain coercive measures against the concessionaire in order to secure observance of the terms of the agreement and removal of the cause of breach.

The coercive measures which are envisaged by certain agreements are:

(1) The prohibition of exportation of petroleum or products by the concessionaire; or

(2) The impounding of the proceeds of sale of petroleum or products.

It will be observed that such coercive measures are envisaged only in cases of default in the payment of amounts due by the concessionaire under the agreement. Some agreements also limit the recourse to such measures to cases where the amounts are payable in accordance with an arbitral decision. Provisions which envisage the taking of coercive measures are found in certain agreements made by Iraq, Iran, Kuwait, Ras Al Khaima and Saudi Arabia.

The earliest provision of such a nature is found in IPC's concession (1925). Article 13 of the concession stated that if the royalties due or awarded by arbitration for any year shall be unpaid for a period of three months after the end of such year, or after the award of the arbitrator, the Government shall have the right to prohibit all export of petroleum and other products until the sum in question is paid. The same Article further provided that if payment be not made within three months after expiration of the aforesaid three months, the Government shall have the right to terminate the convention and to take without payment all the property of the company within Iraq, including the oil collected in the storage tanks and elsewhere.

Iran's agreement with the Consortium provided that if a defined sum of money ordered to be paid in any arbitral decision is not paid within the time limited by such decision or if no time is therein limited, within three months, Iran shall have the right to prohibit all exports of crude oil and petroleum products by the party in default until such sum is paid (Article 45). Another example of the prohibition of exports for breach is found in Kuwait's agreement with Shell (1961). Article 20 of the agreement provided that if the company fails to make payments accruing under the agreement within four months after their due date and the amount of such payments is not in dispute, the Emir shall be entitled, upon giving one month's notice, to prohibit the export of petroleum until the amount in question be paid. If payment be not made within a further period of three months, the Emir shall be entitled to terminate the agreement. A similar provision was included in the agreement between the Ruler of Ras Al Khaima and Kuamco Oil (1962).

The other kind of coercive measure is found in Iran's agreement with Pan American (1958) and in Iran's recent Offshore agreements. Article 42 of the agreement made with Pan American provided that if any final decision or award is given by the arbitration board for payment of money, and such sum is not paid within the time prescribed, or if no time is prescribed, within three months, the Iranian Government shall have the right to require the impounding of the proceeds from all sales or exports of petroleum from Iran by Pan American until such sum is paid. Iran's Offshore agreements (1965) provide in Article 40 that in the case of such default the Government shall have the right to require the impounding of all properties belonging to the debtor as well as the proceeds from all sales or exports of petroleum from Iran by such debtor until the sum is paid.

The recent agreement between Saudi Arabia and Auxirap has distinguished between three different kinds of breaches which may be committed by the concessionaire and has envisaged a separate remedy for each of them. If the breach consists in the failure to pay any rents, royalties or income taxes within four months after they become payable, the Government shall have the right to prohibit all exports of petroleum and other products until the amount is paid; if payment is not made within a further period of three months, the Government shall have the right to terminate the agreement and take over, without payment, all the concessionaire's properties inside Saudi Arabia (Article 62). If the breach consists of the concessionaire's failure to carry out any of the "rights of drilling, producing, refining, transportation and marketing", the Government shall have the right to forfeit such rights, provided that in default of agreement on this question, the issue shall be settled by the procedure laid down in the agreement for the settlement of disputes (Article 64). Finally, if the breach is one for which no provision is made in the agreement or in the income tax law, the penalty shall be damages (Article 65).

SECTION 20. RIGHTS OF GOVERNMENT IN CASE OF EMERGENCY

Most conventions provide for certain exceptional rights in favour of the Government in the case of a national emergency.

IPC's convention provided that on the occasion of a state of emergency (of which the Government shall be the sole judge) the company shall use its utmost endeavours to increase the supply of petroleum and products for the Government's own consumption to the extent the Government shall require. Moreover, the Government shall have the right, while at war with another nation, to use the company's railways and other means of transportation, bridges, wharves, telegraphs and telephones within Iraq on payment of fair compensation.

AIOC's convention stated that if the Government requires utilization of the means of transportation and communication of the company for national defence or in other critical circumstances, it undertakes to impede as little as possible the operations of the company and to pay fair compensation for all damages caused by such utilization.

Aramco's concession stated that in times of national emergency the use of the company's transportation and communication facilities by the Government shall entitle the company to fair compensation for any loss it may sustain thereby, whether through damages to the company's facilities, equipment or installations or through the obstruction or interference with the company's operations.

KOC's convention stated that in times of national emergency the Sheikh shall have the full use free of charge of the company's wireless and telegraphic installations and railways for Governmental purposes. Identical provisions are found in Kuwait's agreements with Aminoil and Arabian Oil Company.

Getty's concession stated that in the event of a national emergency resulting from war, threat of war, insurrection or critical shortage of petroleum products for local consumption, the Government may requisition its needs in this respect from the company and, if the company is unable to meet such needs from its current production, the Government may call upon the company to increase its production. The Government shall reimburse the company for the fair value of any products or property requisitioned. Saudi Arabia's agreement with Japan Petroleum Trading Company contained an identical clause.

The U.A.R.'s agreements with Phillips and Pan American provided that in cases of national emergency due to war or imminent expectation of war or to internal causes, the Government may requisition all or a part of the petroleum production and require EGPC and Phillips to increase such production to the utmost possible maximum. The Government may also requisition the oil field itself, and, if necessary, related processing plants and refineries, if any. The agreements have provided for the indemnification of the concessionaires with respect to damages resulting from any requisition.

SECTION 21. TERMINATION

Oil concessions invariably contain provisions governing their termination otherwise than by effluxion of time. Cases of termination vary. We have already discussed termination of the agreement by the concessionaire under a power of abandonment or surrender reserved under its terms. In discussing breach and its consequences, we have noted the Government's power of termination for breach. We shall, therefore, restrict the discussion here to some provisions relating to termination which are of legal interest.

The Iranian oil agreements envisage their termination if at the end of twelve years of exploration no commercial result has been obtained. This is in application of Article 7 of the Iranian Petroleum Act.

Unless the parties otherwise agree, agreements made with Iran can come to an end only by a decision of the arbitral board or sole arbitrator that they have been terminated by breach or dissolved by total impossibility of performance and in case of breach, only after such arbitral board or sole arbitrator has first prescribed a period of not less than 90 days for compliance with the arbitral decision or award.[5] The earliest provision in this regard was laid down in Article 26 of AIOC's concession (1933). This Article stated that, "This concession can only come to an end in the case that the company should surrender the concession or in the case that the Arbitration Court should declare the concession annulled as a consequence of default of the company in the performance of the present agreement."

The Consortium's agreement with Iran breaks new ground by providing for dissolution of the agreement in the case of total impossibility of performance. Article 41 stipulates that, unless the parties otherwise agree, the agreement shall not be terminated or dissolved prior to the expiration of its terms except by an arbitral decision that it has been terminated by breach or dissolved by total impossibility of performance. The agreement further provided in Article 47 that nothing contained therein (concerning events beyond the reasonable control of any party which render impossible or hinder performance) shall prevent any party from referring to arbitration the question of whether or not the agreement should be dissolved by total impossibility of performance. AGIP's agreement with Iran embodies a similar provision enabling the arbitration panel to declare the invalidity of the agreement by reason of total impossibility of performance (Article 39). It may be observed that the two subsequent agreements made with Pan American and Sapphire do not include any such provision. However, Iran's Offshore agreements of January 16, 1965 have reintroduced the stipulation found in the Consortium's agreement stating that the provisions concerning *force majeure* shall not prevent the other party from referring to arbitration the question of whether or not the agreement should be dissolved

---

[5] See Articles 41C and 45C (3) of the Consortium's agreement (1954) and Article 40 of the Iranian Offshore agreements (1965).

by total impossibility of performance (Article 36). The introduction of the principle of impossibility of performance in oil concessions is an interesting development, especially if one remembers that the same principle has encountered, and in some cases still encounters, difficulty in establishing itself in certain legal systems.

The U.A.R.'s practice with respect to termination of oil agreements materially differs from that followed in Iran. The agreement with Phillips, for example, provides that the Government shall have the right to cancel the agreement by order or decree, with respect either to EGPC or to Phillips, in the following instances:

(i) If the company knowingly has submitted any false statements to the Government which were a material consideration for the execution of the agreement;

(ii) If it fails to pay the rental or royalty within three months from the date of receipt of a written notice from the Government specifying such failure;

(iii) If it assigns any interests contrary to the provisions contained in the agreement;

(iv) If it is adjudicated bankrupt by a court of competent jurisdiction;

(v) If it does not comply with any decision reached by an appropriate U.A.R. court in the event that it becomes necessary to submit to such court any dispute which may arise under the agreement between the parties and which does not have to be submitted to arbitration as provided in the agreement;

(vi) If it intentionally extracts any mineral other than petroleum not authorized by the agreement without the authority of the Government, except such extractions as may be unavoidable as the result of operations conducted in accordance with accepted petroleum industry practice and of which the Department of Fuels shall be notified as soon as possible;

(vii) If it commits any material breach of the agreement or of the provisions of Law No. 66 of 1953, as amended by Law No. 86 of 1956[6] to the extent that such provisions are not superseded by the express provisions of the agreement or of the Law by which the agreement is authorized.

---

[6] Those laws govern mining and quarries and include the petroleum legislation of the U.A.R.

Such cancellation shall take place without prejudice to any rights
which may have accrued to the Government against EGPC or Phillips
in accordance with the provisions of the agreement. In the event of
such cancellation, Phillips shall have the right to remove from the
territory all its personal property. Identical provisions in this respect
are found in the agreements made with Pan American in 1963 and
1964.

SECTION 22. USE OR ACQUISITION OF LAND

As a rule concessions make provision for the concessionaire's right
to acquire either the use or ownership of land, whether State or
private, which is required for his operations.

D'Arcy's concession provided that the Government grants gratu-
itously to the concessionaire all uncultivated lands belonging to the
State which may be necessary for the concessionaire's works. As for
cultivated lands belonging to the State, the concessionaire must purchase them at the fair and current price of the province. The Government also granted to the concessionaire the right of acquiring all or
any other lands or buildings necessary for the same purpose with the
consent of the proprietors on such conditions as may be arranged
between them without the owners being allowed to make demands
of a nature to surcharge the prices ordinarily current for lands situate
in their localities.

The Iraq-IPC convention provided that State lands required for
the concessionaire's undertaking shall be leased to the concessionaire
at a rent of two annas per hectare per annum in the case of uncul-
tivable land and at a fair rent in the case of cultivable land. Lands
not belonging to the Government shall be acquired by the company
from the person concerned or, failing agreement, by the procedure
for acquisition of lands required for a work of public utility.

Subsequent concessions contained more or less similar provisions
regarding the acquisition of land by the concessionaire. It will be
sufficient to refer to the provisions of agreements recently concluded
in Iran and the U.A.R. as typical of the procedure now followed with
respect to the use or acquisition of land by the oil concessionaire.

Pan American's agreement with Iran provided that IPAC—the
subsidiary company created by NIOC and Pan American for the

purpose of exploitation—shall have the right as agent of the parties to the exclusive use without charge of any unutilized lands belonging to the Government which may reasonably be required for use in connection with the operations authorized by the agreement. In the case of utilized land belonging to the Government, its acquisition shall be made upon payment of a reasonable price or rental to the Government. Where land required by IPAC is privately owned, its purchase or lease shall be effected by direct negotiation with the owner. If no agreement is reached, resort may be made to the procedure of land acquisition prescribed in the statutes of NIOC. Provision was also made for the acquisition by IPAC of rights in or over land less than the right to exclusive use, such as easements, right of way and right to construct roads, railroads, pipelines or perform similar works.

The U.A.R.'s concession to Phillips stipulated that the Government shall provide to EGPC and Phillips free of cost all land and rights to land which may be required by them for operations under the concession. In the case of land privately owned, the concessionaire shall pay the reasonable market price or a reasonable rental.

SECTION 23. USE OF NATIONAL TANKERS

A provision requiring the concessionaire to give preference to national tankers has been included in certain recent concessions.

The agreement made between Saudi Arabia and Japan Petroleum Trading Company stated that if the tankers of the company are not at any time sufficient to transport petroleum or products, first preference shall be given for such transportation to tankers owned by the Government or Saudi Arab subjects, provided the rates and terms are substantially the same as those for similar tankers.

The agreement between NIOC and Pan American also provided that the concessionaire will give preferential consideration to the transport of crude oil and products on Iranian flag tankers. The Iranian Offshore agreements of January 16, 1965 have envisaged that the parties will from time to time review the possibility of chartering Iranian owned tankers which are available for worldwide trading, provided they are offered at competitive rates and conditions and are of suitable size, specification and delivery date.

The Kuwait-Shell agreement stipulated that the company will, when in the market to charter tankers, charter at least one tanker flying the Kuwaiti flag and beneficially owned as to a majority by Kuwaiti nationals if suitable for the company's requirements and if available at the market rates and conditions prevailing at the time of charter. The company will also give favourable consideration to the employment, at such rates and conditions, of further tankers of Kuwaiti ownership.

Saudi Arabia's agreement with Auxirap required the company which is to be jointly formed by the parties to use its own tankers or to give preference to Saudi owned tankers in the case of CIF sales, provided the rates and terms are effectively the same as those for similar tankers in a free freight market. This provision does not apply to FOB sales.

Chapter IV

Government Participation in the Oil Industry

Government participation in the oil industry takes the form of participation in profits, management and exploitation.

We have already considered Government participation in the profits of oil companies in discussing the taxation or equal sharing of profits.

We shall now examine the two remaining aspects of Government participation in the oil industry.

SECTION 1. GOVERNMENT PARTICIPATION IN MANAGEMENT

Modest attempts were made in early concessions to establish some contact between the Government and the management of the concessionaire's enterprise. Thus, in the D'Arcy concession, the Government reserved the right to appoint a commissioner who shall be consulted by the concessionaire. AIOC's concession in 1933 stated that the Government had the right to appoint a representative to obtain from the company all information available to stockholders and to attend meetings of the Board of Directors and of stockholders convened to consider questions arising out of the relations between the Government and the company. The Government representative was also empowered to request that such meetings of the Board of Directors be convened at any time to consider any Government proposal. Aminoil's concession in the Neutral Zone (1948) reserved the right of the Sheikh of Kuwait to appoint a representative who will have access to production records and will be entitled to attend Board meetings at which the Sheikh's interests were discussed.

IPC's concession (1925) went a step further. It reserved the right of the Government to appoint to the Board of the company a director who shall enjoy the same rights and privileges as the other directors.

Since the middle of the century, it has become almost a generally recognized practice for Governments of producing countries to nominate one or two representatives to the Board of Directors of oil companies.

Aramco, for example, agreed with the Saudi Arabian Government that the latter shall have the right to nominate two members of the Board of Directors.

The Consortium's agreement with Iran recognized that the Iranian Government shall have the right to be represented on management. It was agreed that the Board of Directors of each of the two Operating Companies formed by the Consortium members for the purpose of implementing the agreement shall consist of seven directors and that no increase will be made in the number of directors in either Board without the consent of Iran. The Consortium members undertook that two of the members of the Board of each company shall be nominated by NIOC.

The right of Government to be represented on management was also stipulated in the Offshore agreements concluded with Arabian Oil Company. The latter's agreement with Saudi Arabia—made originally with Japan Petroleum Trading Company—recognized the Government's right to appoint one member of the Board of Directors. The agreement made between the same company and the Sheikh of Kuwait recognized the right of the Sheikh to nominate one-sixth of the Board of Directors (with a minimum of two) of the company exploiting the concession.

The agreement between Kuwait and Shell stated that the Emir shall have the right to appoint a representative who shall be entitled to attend Board meetings at which the Emir's interests are discussed.

The Hadramaut-Pan American agreement gave the two Governments concerned the right to nominate one-fourth of the Board of Directors of the company with a minimum of two.

Mecom's recent agreement with Jordan reserved the Government's right to appoint one director to the Board of any company formed by Mecom to conduct his activities under the agreement.

The Franco-Algerian Agreement on Hydrocarbons (1965) recognized the Algerian Government's right to appoint one director to the Board of certain concessionary companies.

The Governments of oil producing countries have generally exercised their right to be represented on executive management as indicated above.

SECTION 2. GOVERNMENT PARTICIPATION IN OIL EXPLOITATION

Government participation in oil exploitation can be considered as one of the major developments in the oil industry in the Middle East during the last few years. It has evolved from symbolic to actual participation on a partnership basis. In some countries, Government participation has become either by law or in practice a condition of the grant of oil concessions.

We shall now trace the process of such evolution.

Until very recent times, the terms of almost all oil concession agreements recognized a contingent right of participation by the nationals of the producing country by way of acquisition of stock if and when the concessionaire set up a corporation for exploitation of the concession and issued shares to the public for that purpose. Instances of such provisions are frequent in early concessions. IPC's concession (1925) provided that whenever an issue of shares is offered by the company to the general public, subscription lists shall be opened in Iraq simultaneously as lists are opened elsewhere and Iraqis in Iraq shall be given a preference to the extent of at least 20% of such issue. AIOC's concession (1933) provided that whenever the company shall make issues of shares to the public, the subscription lists shall be opened at Teheran at the same time as elsewhere. It may be remarked that these provisions never resulted in the acquisition by the nationals of producing countries of any part of the stock of an oil company in the manner envisaged by those agreements since no shares have been offered to the public.

There existed, however, two instances where the Government did acquire some of the oil company's stock as part of the consideration for the grant of the concession. The first instance is afforded by the D'Arcy concession. It gave the Persian Government the right to £.St. 20,000 in paid-up shares of the first company founded for the working of the concession. The second instance is found in Aminoil's concession in the Neutral Zone: the concession required the company to offer to the Ruler, with no financial contribution on his part, 15% of the shares of a subsidiary company to be organized for the purpose of exploration and exploitation and 15% of the shares of a subsidiary to be formed for the construction and operation of a refinery.

In more recent agreements the option to participate in the concessionaire's capital stock is not made dependent any longer upon any offer by the concessionaire of a public subscription of shares—an eventuality which is obviously within the concessionaire's entire discretion—but such option is made firmly in favour of Government and conditionally upon the discovery of oil. There exist several instances of such participation options.

Thus, the agreement between Saudi Arabia and Japan Petroleum Trading Company (1957) provided that, after the discovery of oil in commercial quantities, the company undertakes that any company to which the concession has been or will be assigned shall offer for subscription to the Government shares of its capital stock for cash to the extent of 10% of the paid-up capital. The Government shall have the right within 60 days after receipt of such offer from the company to subscribe for itself or for Saudi Arabian subjects to the shares so offered.[1] Such provision shall apply also to any subsequent issue of shares. A somewhat similar provision exists in Kuwait's agreement with Arabian Oil Company (1958).

The Kuwait-Shell agreement (1961) also provided that within a period of 90 days from the date upon which crude petroleum is discovered in commercial quantities, the Emir may elect either by himself or by a Kuwaiti company to take an interest of 20% or less in the venture. The Kuwaiti participant shall pay for such interest in the venture a sum equal to 20% of the total expenditure incurred by the company up to the discovery date. With effect from that date the Kuwaiti participant shall share in the assets and liabilities of the venture in accordance with the Kuwaiti participant's interest therein.

The agreement between the Governments of the two Sultanates of Qu'aiti and Kathiri in Hadramaut and Pan American (1961) embodied a similar provision. It stipulated that any time within the

---

[1] Saudi Arabia has exercised its right to take a 10% interest in this concession.

period commencing with the discovery date and terminating one year after the date of commencement of exports, the two Governments shall have the option to acquire a 20% undivided interest in the company's rights and obligations under the agreement or such a lesser interest as the Governments may elect. The agreement further provided that the Governments shall pay to the company an amount equal to the participation percentage of the sum of all costs and expenses paid or incurred by the company in connection with the concession agreement and operations thereunder up to the participation date.

Under the agreement between the Ruler of Ras Al Khaima and Kuamco Oil (1962), the Sheikh may, within 90 days from the date of the discovery of oil in commercial quantities, elect to take an interest of 20% or less in the venture. In such event, the parties will consult together and agree upon the appropriate corporate structure necessary to promote their interests in the venture. It is further provided that the Sheikh shall pay a sum equal to 20% of the total expenditure incurred by the company up to the date of discovery.

The next step in the evolution was actual Government participation in oil production as distinct from optional participation. Diverse factors have urged some Middle East Governments into the oil industry. In some cases, it is nationalism that aims at the development of national industry. In others, it is socialism that seeks State ownership and exploitation of public resources. In other cases, it is capitalism in search of opportunities for investment.

Government participation in the oil industry now takes two main forms: direct exploitation by the State or exploitation in partnership or in association with a private enterprise.

The system of direct State exploitation can be exclusive or non-exclusive. The system of exclusive State exploitation of petroleum was applied by Turkey in 1929 and by Iran in 1951 when as a result of its dispute with AIOC it nationalized the oil industry—only to be abandoned by both of them in 1954. In that year, Turkey ended its monopoly of the oil business and promulgated Law No. 6326 of March 7, 1954 which was designed to encourage the investment of foreign capital. Also in the same year, Iran reached agreement with a Consortium of oil companies for the operation of its oil resources in the southwest of the country. The only other country in the Middle

East which has adopted a State monopoly of the oil business is Syria. Since 1964 there exists in Syria a prohibition under Legislative Decree No. 133 of December 22, 1964 against the grant of any concession for the exploitation of mineral or petroleum resources.

Excluding Syria, all oil producing countries which engage at present in oil exploitation do so on a non-exclusive basis. Thus, although Turkey and Iran have abandoned the system of exclusive State exploitation of petroleum, they did not abandon oil activities. They still conduct their own independent oil operations. In Egypt also the State engages in direct oil exploitation. Kuwait, Iraq and Saudi Arabia have also made plans to engage in oil operations through national oil companies.

Actual Government participation in the oil industry in partnership with a private enterprise was initiated by Iran in 1957 by its agreement with AGIP. Since then Government participation has become almost the general pattern of new concessions.

Government participation in the oil industry assumes three main forms. These are:

A. Government participation in the capital stock of the concessionary company.

B. Government association with a corporation
   (1) in oil production;
   (2) in integrated oil operations.

C. Association between two Governments: The Franco-Algerian Cooperative Association.

A. GOVERNMENT PARTICIPATION IN THE CAPITAL STOCK OF THE CONCESSIONARY COMPANY

Excluding two minor instances already mentioned of Government participation in the capital stock of concessionary companies (D'Arcy and Aminoil)—such participation constituting part of the consideration for the grant of those two concessions—participation by the Governments of producing countries in the capital stock of concessionary companies has not been extensive. The Egyptian Government owned 9% of Anglo-Egyptian Oil Fields and this participation was increased to 55% in 1961. In Algeria, the Algerian Government and BRP, a French State owned company, held an equal participation of 40.5% each in the capital stock of the *Société de Recherche et d'Exploitation des Pétroles en Algérie*—SN REPAL. By the Franco-Algerian Agreement on Hydrocarbons (1965) Algeria's participation in SN REPAL was raised to 50%. In exercise of its participation option under the concession agreement, Saudi Arabia acquired a 10% interest in the capital stock of Arabian Oil Company.

By far the largest Government participation in the capital stock of oil concessionary companies occurs on the part of foreign Governments, principally the British,[2] French[3] and Italian[4] Governments. All those Governments participate in the capital of certain oil companies which operate in the Middle East and North Africa.

Where the producing country merely owns a share in the stock of the oil company, its interest as a stockholder is merged in the corporate structure. This is in contrast to a partnership between the oil company and the producing country in which a certain degree of separateness is maintained between the respective interests of the parties. In the former case, the relationship is one between stockholders of a corporation while in the latter case the relationship is one between partners of a joint enterprise.

B. GOVERNMENT ASSOCIATION WITH A CORPORATION

The Government of a producing country may be associated in oil production only or it may be associated in integrated operations which cover the production, transportation, refining and marketing of oil.

---

[2] The British Government was the major shareholder of AIOC and is now the major shareholder in British Petroleum Company which in turn possesses shareholding interests in IPC and associated companies.

[3] The French Government holds over one-third of the shares of the *Compagnie Française des Pétroles* which possesses shareholding interests in IPC and Abu Dhabi Marine Areas Ltd. The French Government also participates in the oil industry through two State owned corporations: the *Bureau de Recherches de Pétrole*—BRP and the *Régie Autonome des Pétroles*—RAP. Both are French public companies possessing an industrial and commercial character and are endowed with legal personality and financial autonomy. They are financed by public funds and exercise various functions in relation to the oil industry. In 1964 BRP participated in the capital stock of 27 companies, almost half of which operated in Algeria: see *Annuaire Pétrole Informations* 1964, p. 180. By decrees dated December 17, 1965 BRP and RAP were combined into one public organization possessing an industrial and commercial character called *Entreprise de Recherches et d'Activités Pétrolières*—ERAP.

[4] ENI and its subsidiary AGIP are Italian national companies.

(1) *Government Association in Oil Production*

Government association with a private corporation in oil production exists now in several countries and assumes two main forms: either an unincorporated joint venture or the joint ownership of an operating company. Except in the case of the NIOC-AGIP agreement (1957) and the NIOC-ERAP agreement (1966) both of which will be examined hereinafter, under all forms of association now in existence between oil companies and producing countries with respect to oil production and regardless as to whether the association assumes the form of an unincorporated joint venture or the joint ownership of an operating company, the activities of the association are limited to the search for, and production of, crude oil. Subject to (i) any royalty taken in kind, (ii) the supply of any portion earmarked for internal requirements and (iii) any overlifting and underlifting arrangements between the parties, the crude oil produced is shared at well-head between the parties and taken by them in kind.[5] From the time of the division of the crude oil produced, the partnership relation ceases usually in principle. The division of the crude oil produced between the parties is the principal feature which in practice distinguishes this form of association from a mere shareholding interest in the oil company.

We shall now proceed to consider two typical forms of Government association with a private enterprise in oil production which are in use in the Middle East, particularly in Iran and in the U.A.R.

---

[5] Regarding the division of the crude oil produced see, for example, Article 23 of the Iranian Offshore agreements which states that "petroleum produced shall be owned at the well-head (50%) by First Party and (50%) by Second Party"; Article 17 of the U.A.R.-Phillips agreement which provides that EGPC and Phillips shall each own and have the right to receive, in the proportion of 50%, all the crude oil produced"; Article 14 of the two concessions of Pan American from the U.A.R. which states that "EGPC and Pan American each shall always have the right to take in kind, own and separately dispose of its part of the petroleum produced and saved under this agreement"; Articles 1 and 93 of the Protocol annexed to the Franco-Algerian Agreement on Hydrocarbons which envisage the sharing of the crude oil produced between the parties in accordance with their respective rights in each deposit. In contrast to the practice now prevailing regarding the taking in kind by the parties of the crude oil produced under a joint venture arrangement, Article 12 of the NIOC-AGIP agreement charged SIRIP, the company formed under the agreement, with the duty to sell the petroleum produced first to the parties and, if not bought by them or either of them, to other purchasers.

THE IRANIAN PARTICIPATION FORMULA

Iran's policy with regard to State participation in the oil industry was set out in its Petroleum Act. By this Act NIOC was authorized to participate either in a "mixed organization", meaning a corporation owned in part by NIOC and in part by the other participant, or in what is described in the Act as a "joint structure", that is to say, an operating organization or joint venture created by NIOC and one or more persons but not possessing a separate juridical personality (Article 1).

In accordance with the provisions of this Act, NIOC concluded participation arrangements with several companies: in 1957 it formed a "mixed organization" with AGIP and in 1958 it entered into "joint structures" with Pan American and Sapphire. In January 1965 Iran entered into "joint structures" with five groups of oil companies for offshore operations.

We shall now examine the principal terms of the NIOC-AGIP agreement[6] in more detail than the others because it was the first of its kind and, therefore, set the general pattern of Government participation in the oil industry with a private enterprise.

The agreement provided in Article 1 that the parties will form a company which will exercise on their behalf activities relating to the exploration, operation and sale of crude oil and products. The company so formed was named *Société Irano-Italienne des Pétroles*— SIRIP. Both NIOC and AGIP agreed to subscribe each to 50% of SIRIP's original capital stock fixed at 10,000,000 Rials. Such capital stock could be increased when needed. SIRIP had the power to borrow but if it failed to borrow, NIOC and AGIP each undertook to supply half of the funds required. The two parties were equally represented on management: it was stipulated that the Board of Directors will be constituted 50% of AGIP and 50% of NIOC, the chairman to be appointed by NIOC and the vice-chairman to be appointed by AGIP (Article 4). In order to ensure the smooth running of SIRIP and avoid a deadlock in management by reason of the equal voting power of the parties, each party bound itself to deposit with a

---

[6] For historical reasons and because of the difficulties with AIOC, an inhibition has developed in Iran regarding the use of the term "concession". In Iran an oil concession is described as an oil agreement.

Swiss bank shares to the amount of 1% of the share capital, such deposit to take place under the joint signatures of the parties and under an irrevocable power of attorney. The bank would bind itself to issue admittance cards to general assemblies of the company in respect of such shares to a person appointed by agreement between NIOC and AGIP (Article 6).

The agreement stated that three areas in Iran will be leased to SIRIP to carry out exploration and operations for a term of 25 years from the date on which the sale of petroleum begins with three possible extensions of 5 years each. If no commercial result is obtained at the end of 12 years the agreement will expire and SIRIP will be wound up.

Article 26 of the agreement required the progressive relinquishment of the area of the concession. At the end of the fifth year the original area will be reduced by 25%; at the end of the ninth year the area will be reduced by another 25%; at the end of the twelfth year SIRIP will retain only land in which commercial deposits have been discovered.

In accordance with Article 19, AGIP undertook to assume exploration operations and to spend thereon a total of U.S. $22,000,000 broken down as follows: $6,000,000 in the first four years and $16,-000,000 at a minimum rate of $2,000,000 per year for the next eight years. If at the end of four years the entire $6,000,000 have not been spent, the balance will be added to the minimum expenditure rate for the eight following years. If over-expenditures are made in the first four years, the amount overspent is to be deducted from that required to be expended during the eight following years.

When the existence of an oil deposit sufficient to warrant commercial operation shall have been established, SIRIP shall support any expenditure incurred thereafter for the purpose of developing and operating the said deposit. AGIP's expenditure on exploration shall be refundable if oil is found in a commercially recoverable quantity; if not, such expenditure shall be borne solely by AGIP. The reimbursement of exploration expenses by SIRIP to AGIP shall be made in the following manner: SIRIP shall enter to the credit of AGIP a sum equal to the amount of exploration expenditure with effect from the day on which it was incurred. The payment of credited sums in connection with exploration work shall be carried out by SIRIP within a period as short as possible and in any case through any oil payments not less than the equivalent of U.S. $0.10 per barrel of exported crude oil. Fifty percent of the amount credited to AGIP as refund for exploration work shall be paid by SIRIP to NIOC. Commenting upon this last provision a United Nations report observed that "in the event of an exploitable discovery, the position would therefore be the same as if the partner had paid the National Company a rent equal to half the exploration costs."[7]

The crude oil produced must be offered by SIRIP to AGIP and NIOC, except such quantity as is required to meet NIOC's demands for domestic consumption in the area adjacent to each deposit, but not in excess of 5% of total output, such quantity to be bought by NIOC at cost plus commission of $0.14 per cubic metre. When neither NIOC nor AGIP is prepared to buy the oil at conditions acceptable to SIRIP, the latter may sell it to other purchasers on terms not less favourable to SIRIP (Article 12). Discounts can be granted when SIRIP deems them necessary. The amount of discounts is to be determined by two SIRIP directors.

The agreement made no provision for the payment of rents or premiums.

SIRIP undertook to pay to the Iranian Government:

(i) Royalty at the rate of $12\frac{1}{2}\%$ of the value at posted price of the crude oil delivered to seaboard for export (Article 8);

(ii) Fifty percent of its net profits after deduction of the value of the royalty (Article 17).

The agreement further embodied various other provisions concerning, *inter alia,* currency, drilling and other works, publication of posted prices, service facilities, labour and arbitration of disputes.

AGIP's agreement with Iran introduced the following practices:

(i) The guarantee by the concessionaire of a minimum amount of expenditure on exploration;

(ii) The assumption by the private partner in a joint venture of the entire burden of expenditure on exploration if no oil were found and produced in commercial quantities;

(iii) In the event of oil discovery and production, the reimbursement of the producing country's share in exploration

---

[7] *Petroleum Exploration,* United Nations, 1962, p. 27.

expenditure out of the proceeds of sale of the crude oil produced;

(iv) The sharing by the concessionaire and the producing country of the benefits of oil discovery by exploitation in partnership or by way of a joint venture;

(v) The raising of the revenue of the producing country from 50% to 75% in the total profits derived from oil production, such 75% being composed as follows:

(a) 50% received by the Government in kind in its capacity as a 50% shareholder or partner in the enterprise; and

(b) 25% received by the Government in its capacity as taxing authority in the form of a 50% tax on the private partner's net profits.[8]

The two other agreements made by Iran with Pan American and Sapphire in 1958 substantially followed the basic pattern set by the AGIP agreement subject, however, to certain variations shortly noted hereinafter.

Pan American's agreement differs from AGIP's agreement principally in the following respects:

(i) The operating company formed by the two parties, named IPAC, is a non-profit company owned 50% by NIOC and 50% by Pan American. The two parties subscribe equally to its capital. IPAC acts as agent for either of the parties or for

---

[8] It may here be remarked that, although the difference between the traditional concession system and the system of Government association with a private enterprise under a joint venture arrangement has been commonly expressed in terms of 50-50 and 75-25 sharing respectively, it would seem that the translation of the financial results of such systems in terms of mathematical ratios may be deceptive and could constitute an oversimplification. The system of Government participation in oil exploitation with a private enterprise is another, though extended, application of the 50-50 sharing concept; instead of sharing net profits only, the parties also share the oil. In fact, two sharing arrangements are combined: a 50-50 sharing of the crude oil produced and a 50-50 sharing of the profits derived by the private partner from his share of the crude oil. Although it has been said that such overall sharing results—on the assumption of a 50% Government participation—in a Government-company ratio of 75-25, yet such arrangement requires the Government to provide its 50% share of the capital, usually if and when oil is found in commercial quantities.

both (Article 5). The basic legal difference between the operating company created under the NIOC-AGIP agreement and the operating company established under the NIOC-Pan American agreement is that the former possesses juridical personality, is charged with the sale of the oil produced, realizes a profit and is liable to income tax while the latter is a non-profit organization not vested with a separate juridical personality, is created for the effectuation of a joint venture and is not liable to income tax, such liability falling on the participants to the joint venture;

(ii) The agreement did not provide for the payment of any royalty;

(iii) The agreement provided for payment of annual rent commencing with the 13th year[9] at progressively rising rates of $400 per square kilometre and reaching $600 per square kilometre in the 23rd and subsequent years;

(iv) Pan American agreed to pay NIOC the sum of U.S. $25,000,000 as a cash bonus which can be amortized after commercial production at the rate of 10% annually (Articles 30 and 31);

(v) Pan American undertook to spend a minimum of U.S. $82,000,000 on exploration during a period of 12 years. If oil is discovered by the end of the 12th year and the minimum of U.S. $82,000,000 has not been spent, Pan American undertook to pay to NIOC one half of the unspent balance. The agreement contained provisions similar to those laid down in the agreement between NIOC and AGIP regarding the recoupment of exploration expenses. The agreement similarly provided that 50% of the sums paid to Pan American in repayment of exploration expenses shall be paid by IPAC to NIOC (Article 30);

(vi) IPAC, acting as a non-profit making agent, is not liable to taxation nor does the joint relationship between the parties entail any tax obligation. Tax liability falls upon NIOC and Pan American separately: both are subject to taxation in accordance with the Iranian income tax laws as they may prevail from time to time. It was provided, however, that the rates of

---

[9] During the first twelve years the private partner bears the exploration burden.

tax governing the respective Iranian income tax liability of each party shall not exceed the maximum rate of 50% as provided in the Income Tax Act of 1956 (Articles 5 and 31).

The agreement made between NIOC and Sapphire (1958) was almost identical in terms, though not in figures, to that made with Pan American.[10]

The new Iranian Offshore agreements made in 1965 with six oil groups (Atlantic, French, ENI, Tidewater Oil, Royal Dutch Shell and Deutsche Erdoel-Aktiengesellschaft) follow substantially the same pattern and apply the participation formula set forth above subject to certain differences that we shall presently note.

NIOC and each of the six groups enter into a "joint structure" relationship which does not constitute a separate juridical personality. The parties participate equally in such "joint structure" (Article 2). The "joint structure" acts through an Iranian joint-stock company which is a non-profit corporation and which carries out for their joint account the operations specified in the agreement, except in the case of exploration operations which the operating company will carry out as agent of the foreign participant only (Article 5). Each of the parties undertakes to subscribe and pay for half of the capital stock of the operating company. The equal participation of the parties in the capital stock of the operating company is reflected in its management and each party nominates one half of the members of the Board of Directors (Article 6). At general meetings, each share carries one vote. In the case of equality of voting on any issue at such meetings, the issue shall be deferred once only for further consideration at a subsequent meeting; if, after the adoption of such procedure, there is still an equality of voting then Article 12 of the Petroleum Act applies. This Article provides that in order to ensure that a majority

---

[10] The Sapphire agreement was terminated in 1961 by NIOC as a result of a dispute between the parties with respect to exploratory works. Sapphire suggested the settlement of the dispute by arbitration which NIOC refused. On the basis of the arbitration clause contained in the agreement, Sapphire applied to the President of the Swiss Federal Tribunal for the appointment of a sole arbitrator. NIOC disputed the validity of the arbitrator's appointment and failed to appear in the arbitration proceedings. The arbitrator proceeded *in absentia* and on March 15, 1963 awarded to Sapphire the sum of $2,650,874 as damages for breach of contract. For a report of the Sapphire arbitration, see J.-F. Lalive, in *Annuaire Suisse de Droit International*, Vol. XIX, p. 273 and in *ICLQ* (1964), p. 987.

is attained at general meetings of "mixed companies" in which the parties have equal shares, each of the parties shall assign the voting right of one of its shares to a third person to be nominated by mutual agreement.

The cash bonuses payable by the six groups total U.S. $190,-000,000. Additional bonuses totalling U.S. $51,000,000 become payable after discovery of oil in commercial quantities and production reaches a stated level.

The agreements make a clear distinction between exploration expenditure on the one hand and development and exploitation expenditure on the other hand. The former is borne by the foreign partner alone, while the latter is borne by both parties (Article 15). The foreign partner carries the entire burden of exploration expenditure subject to his right, for income tax purposes, to subtract from his gross receipts in respect of amortization of all such exploration expenditure an amount which is equal to one fifteenth of that expenditure or U.S. $0.10 for each barrel of oil produced and saved, whichever is greater (Articles 12 and 30).

The time at which the exploration operation comes to an end is the date of submission by the foreign partner of a claim for completion of a commercial well. A well is considered "commercial" when evidence indicates that it is capable of producing within a period of twelve years a sufficient volume of petroleum having a value at posted prices that will cover twice the cost of drilling such well. The completion of a commercial well, as defined, does not necessarily establish that the structure is a commercial field. A field is regarded as "commercial" if the quantity of petroleum reasonably foreseen to be produced therefrom can be delivered at seaboard at a profit of not less than 25% of the applicable posted price after deduction from such posted price of the cost of production, including amortization of exploration expenditure, transport and loading charges and a sum equal to $12\frac{1}{2}\%$ of the posted price (Article 15).

All expenditure incurred subsequently to the date of the claim by the foreign participant of the first commercial well discovery until the date of commencement of commercial production—defined in Article 33 as the export of 100,000 cubic metres of petroleum—is considered as development and exploitation expenditure to be borne by both parties. However, the foreign partner undertakes, upon discovery of any commercial field, to provide, in addition to his own share, NIOC's share of the expenditure required for development and exploitation until the date of commencement of commercial production, such share to be reimbursed in installments. Such advance is made either free of interest as in the case of the Royal Dutch-Shell agreement or subject to the payment of interest as in the case of the agreements with Atlantic, Tidewater and Deutsche Erdoel (Article 15).

As from the date of commencement of commercial production, the parties assume the responsibility of all expenditure for all petroleum operations in respect of the field. The same provisions apply in respect of any field discovered subsequently to the first field.

The six groups undertake to expend sums totalling U.S. $130,-000,000 on exploration expenses during the first twelve years.

The petroleum produced is owned at the well-head in equal shares by the two parties which may freely export same without the necessity of a licence or the payment of customs or export taxes (Article 23).

The agreements introduce in Article 22 new provisions with respect to overlifting by one party of a larger quantity than its own share in the petroleum produced. It is stated that each party may take from the operating company one half of the quantity available for export and may purchase any part of the other half which is not taken by its owner. Any party lifting more than its share of 50% in any calendar year is deemed to have purchased from the other party one half of the difference in volume between the respective liftings and shall pay to the other party an amount equal to the volume deemed to have been purchased multiplied by one half of the sum of the following:

(a) The weighted yearly average of the posted price;
(b) The unit production cost;
(c) Any other costs which may, in accordance with taxation regulations, be included in the production cost.

There is no need to refer again to the tax features of these agreements as they have already been mentioned in Chapter II.

In other respects, the Offshore agreements follow fairly closely the pattern and conditions established in prior joint venture agreements made by Iran.

On August 27, 1966 NIOC concluded with ERAP[11] an agreement which departs from the usual pattern followed in previous Iranian oil agreements and from the concept of joint ventures envisaged by the Iranian Petroleum Act.[12] The agreement is made between NIOC and two corporations, ERAP and its subsidiary SOFIRAN.

ERAP undertakes the financing of exploration and development operations. Its advances concerning exploration constitute loans to NIOC repayable without interest within fifteen years if petroleum is discovered and produced in commercial quantities. Advances relating to development constitute loans to NIOC repayable with interest within a period of five years. In addition to its financing function, ERAP will perform commercial services by acting as a broker for the sale on behalf of NIOC of certain quantities of crude oil on world markets. As consideration for services rendered, NIOC guarantees to ERAP the sale, at an agreed price, of a percentage of the oil produced, such percentage varying between 35% to 45% according to the distance of the oilfield from the seaboard.

SOFIRAN is entrusted by NIOC with the exclusive functions of a general contractor. Such functions cover technical services such as exploration, drilling and other acts associated with exploration and production. SOFIRAN's operations are of a non-profit making nature and are not liable to taxation.

The NIOC-ERAP agreement obviously deviates from the usual pattern of joint venture arrangements in application in Iran or elsewhere in the Middle East. Though such agreement is not unlike other joint venture arrangements in the sense that ERAP, in consideration of its providing the risk capital required for oil exploration and the financing needed for development, acquires a right to a percentage of the oil discovered and produced, yet the joint venture contemplated here possesses the following principal particularities:

(1) The percentage of oil production which ERAP is entitled to purchase at the agreed price is substantially less than

---

[11] ERAP is a French State owned corporation which was formed in 1965 as a result of the merger of RAP and BRP which were also two French State owned corporations.

[12] For the English text of the NIOC-ERAP agreement see *Platt's Oilgram News Service*, December 30, 1966.

the 50% share derived by NIOC's partner under other Iranian joint venture arrangements.

(2) The usual right possessed by NIOC's partner under other joint venture arrangements to take its share of the oil *in specie* at well-head is replaced by a contractual right recognized in ERAP's favour to purchase a percentage of the oil produced which is entirely owned at well-head by NIOC.

(3) No part of the functions of ERAP under the agreement entail liability to taxation. It is to be remarked, however, that an amount equivalent to the usual Iranian income tax is wrapped up in the purchase price payable by ERAP to NIOC for crude oil bought. Such purchase price is determined on the basis of cost with the addition of an amount corresponding to 50% of the difference between cost and realized price, the latter being the F.O.B. selling price of crude oil in the Persian Gulf. The agreement provides that this rate of 50% shall be the same as the income tax rate applicable from time to time to companies working in Iran in association with NIOC.

(4) The agreement provides that one half of the recoverable reserves which are discovered shall be set aside as a "national reserve" while the other half only shall be subject to development and commercial exploitation. The allocation to reserves shall be effected only if the first discovered commercial field can cover the reimbursement to ERAP of the total exploration expenses incurred or to be incurred.

(5) The agreement, being one which is made between two state owned corporations, takes into account certain considerations which ordinarily lie beyond the scope of a business contract between two strictly commercial organizations. This is evidenced by the provision in the agreement which envisages the purchase by NIOC and the Iranian Government of French good and services in return for ERAP's undertaking to market certain quantities of the crude oil produced for NIOC's account.

The NIOC-ERAP agreement has been hailed as one which embodies a substantially higher sharing formula than that involved in other joint venture arrangements. Although a comparison between joint venture arrangements involving different elements may lack the precision required for an accurate evaluation yet, as far as one can judge, the agreement may not be as revolutionary as was thought at first. In the absence of royalty payments and because the purchase price formula is related to realized rather than to posted prices, it is estimated that the financial results of the NIOC-ERAP agreement to the producing country and the offtakers do not appear to differ materially from those achieved under other joint venture arrangements.

THE EGYPTIAN PARTICIPATION FORMULA

Until 1956, petroleum exploration and exploitation in the U.A.R. were entirely in the hands of foreign oil companies. In 1956, the Government set up the General Petroleum Authority which was empowered to engage in the whole range of petroleum operations and to possess capital holdings in other organizations. In 1957, the General Petroleum Company was established. The General Petroleum Company is owned by the Government through the Economic Institution, also a Governmental corporation.

In 1963 and 1964, the U.A.R. concluded four agreements for the exploitation of oil resources in partnership between the State owned EGPC and foreign companies. Those agreements were made with Phillips on September 25, 1963; with Pan American on October 23, 1963; with ENI on December 1, 1963 and again with Pan American on February 12, 1964.

We shall now examine the main features of the agreement made with Phillips because it was the prototype followed in other similar concessions in the U.A.R.

There are two concessionaires under the agreement: EGPC and Phillips. The Government granted to EGPC and Phillips, in the proportion of 50% undivided interest to each of the two grantees, an exclusive concession in the Western Desert of Egypt covering an area of about 96,000 square kilometres for a primary term of 30 years from the effective date of the agreement with the right of the grantees to extend the said term for an additional period of 15 years. The rights, duties, obligations and liabilities of the parties under the agreement are several and not joint, "it being the express purpose and intention of the parties that the ownership of their respective percentage interests under the agreement shall be as tenants in common and that no relationship under the agreement shall be construed as constituting an association, corporation, mining partnership or any other kind of partnership" (Article 49).

The agreement provided for the gradual relinquishment of the area of the concession as follows: 1/4 th to be relinquished upon or prior to the expiration of the third year; another 1/4 th to be relinquished upon or prior to the expiration of the sixth year; upon the expiration of the tenth year EGPC and Phillips shall have the right to select and retain, in addition to exploration blocks already converted to development leases or being the subject of an application for this purpose, a number of exploration blocks not to exceed 10% of the original territory covered by the concession.

Phillips agreed that it shall bear and pay all costs and expenses required for exploration operations in an amount of U.S. $10,000,000 broken down as follows: $3,000,000 during the first three years and $1,000,000 in each year from the 4th to the 10th year and a further sum of $25,000 per exploration block during the 11th and 12th years of the concession. After commercial discovery EGPC and Phillips will each bear and pay 50% of all the costs and expenses incurred for development, production, further exploration and all other operations (Article 6). A company, named WEPCO, was to be formed by EGPC and Phillips, to act as the operating company in order to carry out on their behalf development, production and exploration after the date of commercial discovery. EGPC and Phillips would each own one half of the capital stock of the company. WEPCO will not own any right, title or interest in or under the agreement or under any development lease or in any of the petroleum produced or in any of the equipment or other property obtained or used in connection therewith (Article 11).

Except for exploration expenses which are to be borne by Phillips, the parties agreed that each of them will pay and bear 50% of the costs and expenses incurred by WEPCO on their behalf in carrying out joint operations under the agreement.

Each of the parties will own and have the right to receive 50% of all the crude oil produced and can dispose of such crude oil as it sees fit (Article 17).

The concession further provided in Article 14 for a sole risk operations clause. In accordance with this clause, if at any time either EGPC or Phillips shall desire that any exploration, development, production, transportation or other operation be carried out and the other party does not wish to participate therein, then the proposing party is entitled to advance to WEPCO all costs and expenses required for such operation and shall be entitled to have such operation carried out at its sole cost, expense and risk. In such event all petroleum produced and saved as a result of such operation shall belong to the proposing party alone. Under certain terms and conditions and proper indemnification of the proposing party for its costs and expenses, the other party may exercise the right to participate jointly with the proposing party in respect of such sole risk operation.

The agreement provided for payment of rents, royalties and taxes.

In accordance with Article 6 no rent is payable during the period of exploration: the exploration expenditure obligation is considered to be in lieu of rent. As from the time of conversion of an exploration block into a development lease, EGPC and Phillips together undertake to pay to the Government a rental at the rate of £.Eg. 25,000 per annum for each exploration block so converted (Article 21).

Royalty was fixed at 15% of the total quantity of petroleum produced and saved. The Government may take its royalty in kind or in cash, or partly in kind and partly in cash, at its election. The value of the Government's royalty is calculated on the basis of the weighted average export price received for crude oil by EGPC or Phillips from non-affiliated purchasers during the period for which the said royalty is due, such price to be computed back to the main storage tank (Article 21).

The tax provisions embodied in this agreement have already been mentioned while discussing the taxation of profits in Section 5 of Chapter II.

The concession granted by the U.A.R. to Pan American on October 23, 1963 covered an area of about 73,000 square kilometres in Fayoum and Agila. The agreement followed that made between the U.A.R. and Phillips. The grantees were EGPC and Pan American. Pan American undertook to spend U.S. $17,000,000 on exploration. The setting up of an operating company called FAPCO and other obligations were almost identical as in the other agreement. The agreement was made for a term of 30 years, subject to an option to extend such term by 15 years. However, the agreement terminates if at the end of the 12th year there has been no commercial discovery by that date. The relinquishment obligations are similar, though not identical, to those embodied in the agreement with Phillips. Finally, the agreement made provision for the payment of rents, royalties (15%) and taxes (50%).

The agreement between the U.A.R. and ENI made on December 1, 1963 embodied a concession to International Egyptian Oil Company which, upon commercial discovery, shall be transferred to Oriental Petroleum Company of Egypt (COPE). ENI and the Egyptian Government have a 50% interest in COPE. The concession covered an area of about 28,000 square kilometres in the Delta and Gulf of Suez and was made for a period of 30 years. It is renewable for a further term of 15 years. The International Egyptian Oil Company undertook to spend a minimum of U.S. $20,000,000 on exploration. Government receives 50% of the net profits of COPE in the form of royalties, taxes and rentals. The remaining 50% of net profits is divided between the shareholders of COPE. The other provisions of this agreement are similar to the concessions granted to Phillips and Pan American.

The concession granted by the U.A.R. to Pan American on February 12, 1964 related to that part of the Gulf of Suez not under a prior concession and covered an area of about 2,500 square miles. This agreement followed closely the previous agreement made between the same parties in 1963 with respect to the Western Desert. However, the following differences may be noted:

(a) Pan American undertook in the agreement made in 1964 to expend on exploration the sum of U.S. $27,500,000, as follows: $10,000,000 during the first two years and $2,500,000 in each year from the third to the ninth year. From the tenth to the twelfth year, one exploration drilling rig must be continuously operated.

(b) The agreement terminates if at the end of the fourth year or upon the expenditure by Pan American for exploration of the sum of $27,500,000, whichever date is later, there has been no commercial discovery.

(c) The royalty on the total quantity of petroleum produced which is 15% in Pan American's agreement of 1963 is increased to 20% in the later agreement. The provision in this agreement which envisaged the reduction of the royalty to 15% on the happening of certain conditions has been mentioned earlier.[13]

(2) *Government Association in Integrated Oil Operations*

Government association in integrated oil operations extends beyond oil production and includes refining, transportation and marketing. The integration formula has received applications in Persia and Saudi Arabia.

THE SAUDI ARABIAN PARTICIPATION FORMULA

This form of Government participation in the oil industry was originally introduced by the agreement concluded on December 22, 1920 between the Persian Government and the Anglo-Persian Oil Company. This agreement defined the scope of application of the provision in the D'Arcy concession which gave the Government 16% of the net profits of the enterprise. The new agreement settled a controversy between the parties and stated that the Persian Government was entitled to receive 16% of all annual "net profits arising from the mining, refining and marketing of Persian oil whether all the stages of the process were handled by the company itself or through subsidiary companies, whether in Persia or outside" but to the exclusion of profits arising from the transportation of oil by means of ships.[14] This form of profit sharing was abandoned in the revised concession granted to the company on April 29, 1933 as mentioned earlier.[15]

The integration concept was also applied in the concession granted by Saudi Arabia to Japan Petroleum Trading Company (1957). In accordance with Article 5 of the agreement, the company undertook to exercise its rights "as an integrated entity, that is, it shall itself carry out all the operations of an integrated oil enterprise,

---

[13] Section 4 of Chapter II.

[14] B. Shwadran, *The Middle East, Oil and the Great Powers 1959*, 2nd ed., p. 35.

[15] See Section 2A of Chapter II.

including production, refining, transportation and marketing." However, in view of the fact that Saudi Arabia's participation in the equity of the enterprise was limited to 10%, it is evident that such agreement embodied only an embryonic application of the concept of Government participation in integrated oil operations as compared with Saudi Arabia's subsequent agreement with Auxirap.

The agreement with Auxirap, a French State owned public corporation and a subsidiary of RAP, was concluded on April 4, 1965. Another agreement was simultaneously concluded between Auxirap and the General Petroleum and Mineral Organization—Petromin, an organization of the Saudi Arabian State, which created an association between them in order to carry out the operations contemplated by the main agreement made between Saudi Arabia and Auxirap.

Under the terms of the main agreement, Auxirap was granted an exploration and prospecting licence for a period of two years which is renewable under certain conditions for a further period of three years (Articles 1, 3 and 4). The holder of the licence was required to commence exploration and prospecting operations within six months and drilling operations during the second year. Under Article 3, Auxirap was required to spend during the first two years not less than five million dollars on exploration and prospecting operations.

Upon the discovery of oil in commercial quantities, an exploitation concession lease is granted to the holder of the concession (Article 8). Within six months following the grant of such a lease, a Saudi Arabian company will be formed in which a participation of 40% shall be offered for subscription to the Government. The Government may subscribe either for itself or for any of its agencies or for Saudi Arabian subjects. The same right to subscribe is possessed by the Government with respect to issues of new shares in the same percentage as its original subscription. Should the Government decline participation, Auxirap remains the sole owner of the rights and obligations arising under the agreement (Article 9).

The capital of the operating company was fixed at U.S. $20,000,-000 with an initial paid-up capital of U.S. $5,000,000. Exploration expenses and assets at book value will be considered as part of Auxirap's subscription to the capital of the company. When the company is formed, the exploitation concession lease must be transferred to the company (Article 10).

The Saudi participation in the operating company is represented by Petromin. Notwithstanding the inequality of the financial participation of the parties in the capital stock of the company, the Saudi participation and the French participation possess an equal right of representation on management and an equal voting power at general meetings or meetings of the Board of Directors (Article II). The Board of Directors consists of an even number of directors, half of whom, including the Chairman, are appointed by the Saudi Arabian shareholders, while the other half, including the Vice-Chairman, are appointed by the French shareholders. The Chairman does not hold a casting vote. It may be noticed that, unlike the Iranian agreements, no provision is foreseen in the event of a deadlock arising by reason of the equal voting power of the parties.

The company's objects are exploration, exploitation, processing, transportation, refining and marketing of petroleum. Article 26 of the agreement stated that the concessionaire—such term being defined as meaning Auxirap during the exploration and prospecting period and meaning the operating company after the transfer to it of the exploitation concession lease—will, once the company is created, enjoy and exercise the rights mentioned in the agreement as an integrated entity, that is, it shall carry out all operations as an integrated oil enterprise, including production, refining, transportation and marketing of crude oil under the following conditions:

(i) The refining capacity of the integrated entity shall be limited to 50% of the crude oil produced. Such refining capacity should be in operation not later than at the end of the fifteenth year following the granting of the exploitation concession.

(ii) When the company sells CIF, it shall either use its own tankers or give preference to Saudi Arabian tankers. This provision is not applicable to FOB sales.

(iii) The company shall itself market 50% of the crude oil produced not later than at the end of the tenth year, it being understood that the supply of crude oil to the company's refineries shall be included in the said 50% to be marketed.

(iv) As for such part of the company's production which is not used in integrated operations, Auxirap and Petromin assume its sale in proportion to their respective shares in the company. However, Article 27 provides that Auxirap undertakes, if so requested by Petromin, to take over the marketing of the whole or part of Petromin's share of the crude oil produced, subject to a reasonable marketing allowance which shall be agreed upon between the parties and which shall not be taxable in Saudi Arabia.

The agreement makes provision for the payment of bonuses, rentals, royalties and income taxes. The financial and fiscal aspects of the agreement have already been considered in Chapter II. One point may, however, be mentioned here. Unlike the position under the Iranian and Egyptian participation agreements where the stockholders of the operating company pay separately the income taxes due to the Government, here such payments are made by the concessionaire, i.e., the operating company formed by the parties (Article 22). This arrangement follows the precedent set by Iran's agreement with AGIP in 1957 but which was abandoned in subsequent Iranian agreements.

C. Association Between Two Governments: The Franco-Algerian Cooperative Association

This form of association, now named ASCOP, was introduced by the Protocol annexed to the Franco-Algerian Agreement on Hydrocarbons of July 29, 1965 which came into force on December 30, 1965.[16] The Protocol comprises 180 articles and five appendices and constitutes a complete and exhaustive petroleum code covering the activities of the association. Although, in essence, the association resembles in some respects other forms of joint venture arrangements for the production of crude oil in force in the Middle East, yet it possesses distinctive traits, both legal and financial, which give it an individuality of its own. Only a brief outline of the main features of the association can be attempted here.

The object of the association is the exploration and exploitation in common between the French and Algerian Governments of petroleum in Algeria.[17] Although the association was brought into existence

---

16 For the text of the Agreement and Protocol, see *Journal Officiel de la République Française,* December 26, 1965, p. 11793.

17 Except as otherwise provided in the Agreement, companies holding mining titles by virtue of the Sahara Petroleum Code remain subject to the provisions of the said Code and the terms of their concessions. (Article 47 of the Agreement).

by an agreement concluded between the French and Algerian Governments, yet the actual association itself was established between two Government owned companies. The two companies join their efforts for the search and exploitation of hydrocarbons in Algeria, "each party taking its share in the substances produced in kind and at cost" (Article 1 of the Protocol). The two companies consist of an Algerian Company, called "Company A",[18] created by the Algerian State or its public corporations and a French Company, named "Company F", created by BRP and RAP, two French State owned corporations.[19] The contract of association between the two companies was deemed to have been concluded by signature of the Protocol (Article 1 of the Protocol). It is a matter of interest to observe that a contractual relationship entailing various rights and obligations was thus created between two corporations which were not even in existence at the date on which the agreement was signed by the two Governments.

By virtue of Article 23 of the Protocol the two companies acquire an exclusive permit of exploration and exploitation of hydrocarbons in a zone having an area of 180,000 square kilometres named the mining domain. Parcels situated outside the zone and which are the subject of oil concessions may also be brought into the scope of the association under certain conditions detailed in the Protocol. The zone covered by the association is divided into parcels each having an area not exceeding 10,000 square kilometres. The effective entry of each parcel into the mining domain is subject to a contract to be concluded between the two companies. In accordance with Article 41 of the Protocol this contract must be drawn up for each parcel and must specify the delimitation of the parcel, the percentage of participation of each of the parties, an undertaking of performance of works and the designation of the Operator, i.e., the company charged with the management of exploration and development operations of the parcel. The percentage of participation of each party in each parcel shall not be less than 10% for any one parcel provided that the aggregate participation of each party shall be 50% of the

---

[18] The Algerian Company which represents the Algerian State in the Cooperative Association is named "Sonatrach".

[19] Company F has since been constituted under the name of "Sopefal": *Pétrole Informations*, February 20, 1966, p. 11.

total area covered by the association (Article 45).[20] Thus, each parcel
is the subject of a separate contractual, financial and operational enterprise. The formula of the cooperative association in use in Algeria
consists, in effect, of a number of partnerships of unequal participation percentages which result in an overall approximately equal participation by the two parties in the common enterprise.

From the fact that each parcel is the subject of a distinct and
separate contract flows an important legal consequence, namely, in
the event of breach by one party of its undertakings or obligations,
whether towards the other party or towards the Algerian State, which
results in the loss or forfeiture of such party's rights, such loss or
forfeiture applies only to the parcel in respect of which it was incurred and does not affect the relationships existing between the
parties with respect to the other parcels. Thus, Article 58 of the
Protocol which envisages the forfeiture of a party's rights over a parcel
as a result of the breach of certain of its obligations states that forfeiture extends only to the parcel in respect of which it is incurred.
So also the delay or default by one party in the payment of its share
of the expenses affects only the parcel in respect of which the delay
or the default has occurred (Article 69). In other words, a breach
by one party of its obligations with respect to one parcel is not a
breach of the entire contract of association. The severable character
of a breach under the Franco-Algerian Cooperative Association stands
in contrast to the rule generally applicable in contracts, namely, a
breach, though it may relate to a part of the contract, usually constitutes a breach of the whole agreement.

The two companies joined in such Cooperative Association do
not constitute a juristic person nor do they act through an operating
company as in the case of other joint venture arrangements between
producing countries and oil companies. Their relationship remains
that of an unincorporated association governed by the terms and conditions of the Protocol.

The operational aspects of the association substantially differ
from other forms of association. The Cooperative Association acts

---

[20] The latitude given to the parties to possess different participation percentages in different parcels stands in contrast to other forms of Government
association in oil production.

by means of three organs: a Council of Management (*Conseil de Direction*), a Technical Committee and an Operator.

The Council of Management is composed of twelve members chosen in equal numbers by the two companies. Its President is chosen from among the members designated by Company A and its Vice-President from among the members designated by Company F. The Council of Management is entrusted with the management of all the affairs of the association. Decisions are taken by a majority of two-thirds of the members present. If it is not possible to reach the required majority decision, the Council will call in a conciliator. Failing agreement on the choice of a conciliator, the President of the Cantonal Tribunal at Zurich (Switzerland) can be requested by either of the parties to appoint a conciliator. If within forty days from the date of his appointment the conciliator has not succeeded in his mission, the parties may have recourse to arbitration (Article 10 of the Protocol).

The Technical Committee is composed of six members designated in equal numbers by the parties. This Committee deals with such matters as are delegated to it by the Council of Management and makes recommendations to the Council. It decides by a majority of two-thirds of the members present. If it is not possible to attain the required majority, the matter in issue is referred to the Council of Management for its decision (Article 12).

The Operator is one of the two companies, though each party may delegate its functions as Operator to a company which it controls. An Operator is chosen for each parcel. Normally, the Operator will be the party which possesses the higher participation percentage. The parties, however, will attempt to achieve an overall equality between them with respect to the various appointments of Operators required for the whole mining domain. The Operator acts as the manager of the association with respect to the parcel in accordance with the decisions taken by the Council of Management and the Technical Committee (Article 19).

Each of the parties undertakes to meet the expenses required for exploration and exploitation operations in proportion to its participation percentages (Articles 52 and 101 of the Protocol). Any party which fails to finance all or part of its share will lose its rights with respect to the parcel in respect of which default is made (Article 69). However, with respect to certain expenses required for development following an exploitable discovery, Company A is entitled in relation to each parcel to request Company F for an advance equal to the smaller of either 60% of Company A's share in annual exploration expenses with respect to such parcel or the annual amount required from Company F for financing such expenses. Such advances are reimbursed in kind out of a quantity not exceeding one-quarter of Company A's share from the crude oil produced from all deposits in the area covered by the association. For purposes of calculation of the amount to be thus reimbursed, the crude oil taken in kind by way of repayment is valued at the average price for realizations of Company F's normal share (Article 77 of the Protocol). This method of recoupment of development expenses differs from the methods of recoupment of exploration expenses followed in Egypt and Iran.

The parties share the crude oil produced in proportion to their respective interests in the deposit (Articles 1 and 93 of the Protocol). However, any quantity not lifted by the party entitled to it can be bought by the other party at prices equal to average realization prices but progressively discounted at rates ranging from 5 to 20% (Article 95 of the Protocol).

The Agreement is concluded for 15 years and may be extended for an equal period by consent of the two Governments. At the request of one of the parties, it can be revised at the end of 5 years by mutual consent. The Agreement provides that after its expiration the commitments undertaken during its currency with respect to each parcel will continue in force both with respect to exploration and to exploitation (Article 52). The Protocol provides that upon discovery of an oil deposit its area shall be delimitated by the Council of Management and the phase of exploitation which is fixed at a period of 25 years will begin from the date of delimitation. Such period is extended automatically for five years at the request of either of the parties and may be further extended by the Algerian State for another ten years at the joint request of the two parties (Article 34).

Companies A and F are subject to a tax equal to 55% of their profits, provided that the tax shall in no case be less than 1/8th of the value of petroleum at the point of loading or delivery reduced by costs and charges of handling, storage and transportation as from collection points (Article 125 of the Protocol). Regarding certain tax aspects, the Protocol refers to the provisions of the Sahara Petroleum Code (Article 126) while as regards other aspects, it lays down new provisions, such as those relating to the determination of the taxable income (Article 129), the exemption from certain taxes (Article 135) and the limitation of the level of taxes of general application (Article 139).

The Agreement creates three relationships which carry different legal consequences:

(i) a relationship between the French and Algerian States resulting from the agreement made between them;

(ii) a relationship between the two State owned companies joined in Cooperative Association;

(iii) a relationship between Company F and the Algerian Government.

If differences or disputes arise between the parties, the remedies available differ in each case. Disputes between the two States, if not settled by conciliation or arbitration, are referred to the International Court of Justice (Article 51 of the Agreement). Disputes between the two companies or between Company F and the Algerian State, if not settled by conciliation, are referred to the decision of an international arbitration tribunal (Article 157 of the Protocol).

OIL CONCESSIONS AND OIL CONCESSIONAIRES IN THE MIDDLE EAST AND NORTH AFRICA[1]

ABU DHABI

Petroleum Developments (Trucial Coast), Ltd. (now named Abu Dhabi Petroleum Company, Ltd.)

Abu Dhabi Marine Areas, Ltd., 1953

Abu Dhabi Marine Areas, Ltd., Supplemental, 10 November 1966

ADEN/HADRAMAUT

Pan American Hadramaut Oil Company (with Sultanates of Qu'aiti and Kathiri), 5 November 1961

Petroleum Concessions, Ltd. (IPC) (with Aden, including Hadramaut and Socotra Island)

Hadramaut Oil Company

AJMAN

John W. Mecom

ALGERIA

Compagnie de Recherche et d'Exploitation de Pétrole au Sahara (CREPS)

Société Nationale de Recherches de Pétrole en Algérie (SN. REPAL) (since 1965 owned 50% by the Algerian Government and 50% by the Bureau de Recherches de Pétroles, BRP)

Compagnie Francaise des Pétroles–Algérie (CFPA) owned to the extent of 85% by CFP

Compagnie des Pétroles d'Algérie (CPA)

---

[1] The text and sometimes the date of concessions is not always available or published. Hence, this list does not purport to be a complete one. Moreover, with respect to North Africa, the list refers both to holders of search permits as well as to holders of concessions inasmuch as concessions are granted only after commercial discovery.

COPEFA

PETROPAR

SNPA

FRANCAREP

COPAREX

SAFREP

Franco-Algerian Agreement on Hydrocarbons, 29 July 1965

SONATRACH, Société Nationale pour la Recherche, la Production, le Transport, la Transformation et la Commercialization des Hydrocarbures

SOPEFAL

Other Oil Companies in Algeria:

Phillips Petroleum Co. (Algérie)

El Paso

Weedol

Tidewater

Amif

Mobil Sahara

Esso Sahara

BAHRAIN
Eastern and General Syndicate, Ltd., 2 December 1925

Eastern and General Syndicate, Ltd., Assignment to Bapco, 12 June 1930

Bahrain Petroleum Co., Ltd., 29 December 1934

Bahrain Petroleum Co., Ltd., Supplemental, 3 June 1936

Bahrain Petroleum Co., Ltd., Supplemental, 19 June 1940

Bahrain Petroleum Co., Ltd., Voluntary Payments, 28 June 1951

Bahrain Petroleum Co,. Ltd., Supplemental, 8 December 1952

Bahrain Petroleum Co., Ltd., Most Favoured Nations, 8 December 1952

Bahrain Petroleum Co., Ltd., Crude Oil Value for Tax, 8 December 1952

Bahrain Petroleum Co., Ltd., Termination Voluntary Payments, 8 December 1952

Bahrain Petroleum Co., Ltd., Submission to 50/50 Tax, 16 December 1952

DHOFAR

Dhofar-Cities Service Petroleum Corp., 17 January 1953

John W. Mecom—Pure Oil Company

DUBAI

Dubai Marine Areas, Ltd., August 1952 (B.P. and C.F.P.)

Dubai Petroleum Company (subsidiary of Continental Oil Company)

HADRAMAUT

American International Oil Company

IRAN

Anglo-Iranian Oil Co., Ltd., D'Arcy Convention, 28 May 1901

North Iranian Oils, Ltd., Khoohtaria Concession, 9 March 1916

Sinclair Exploration Co., Inc., 20 December 1923

Anglo-Iranian Oil Co., Ltd., 29 April 1933

Amiranian Oil Co. Inc., 3 January 1937

Consortium, 20 September 1954

AGIP Mineraria Company, 3 August 1957

Pan American Petroleum Corporation, 24 April 1958

Sapphire Petroleums, Ltd., June 1958

Offshore agreements were made by the Iranian Government on January 16, 1965 and came into force on February 13, 1965 with the following groups of companies:

The Atlantic Group comprising: Atlantic Refining Co./ Sinclair Oil Corp./Sun Oil Co./Union Oil Company of California/Murphy Oil Corp.

The Tidewater Group comprising: Tidewater Oil Co./Skelly Oil Co./Superior Oil Co./Sunray DX Oil Co./Industries Corp./Kerr-McGee Oil Industries Inc./Cities Service Co./ Richfield Oil Corp.

An International Group comprising: Phillips Petroleum Co./ ENI-AGIP/Indian Oil and Natural Gas Commission.

The French Group comprising: BRP (Bureau de Recherches de Pétroles) /RAP (Régie Autonome de Pétroles) / EURAFREP (Société de Recherche et d'Exploration de Pétroles) /COPAREX (Compagnie de Participation de Recherches et d'Exploitation Pétrolières) /SCRAMCARET (Compagnie Franco-Africaine de Recherches Pétrolières).

Royal-Dutch Shell affiliate named Bataafse Petroleum Maatschappij N.V.

An offshore concession was also granted on June 16, 1965 to a group of German companies comprising Deutsche Erdoel, Deutsche Schachtbau, Gelsenkirchener, Gewerkschaft Elwerath, Preussag, Scholven-Chemie and Wintershall.

IRAQ

Iraq Petroleum Co., Ltd., 14 March 1925

Anglo-Persian Oil Co., Ltd., 24 May 1926, whose concession was taken over by a subsidiary named Khanaqin Oil Company

Iraq Petroleum Co., Ltd., Supplemental, 24 March 1931

Iraq Petroleum Co., Ltd., (Revision of 14 March 1925 Convention and Supplemental of 24 March 1931), 7 April 1932

Mosul Petroleum Co., Ltd., BOD Convention, 20 April 1932

Basrah Petroleum Co., Ltd., 29 July 1938

Iraq Petroleum Co., Ltd.   )
Mosul Petroleum Co., Ltd.   )   Agreement, 3 February 1952
Basrah Petroleum Co., Ltd.)

Iraq Petroleum Co., Ltd.   )
Mosul Petroleum Co., Ltd.   )   Letters, 3 February 1952
Basrah Petroleum Co., Ltd.)

JORDAN

Iraq Petroleum Co., Ltd., 11 January 1931

Anglo-Iranian Oil Co., Ltd., 26 September 1933

Iraq Petroleum Co., Ltd., 8 February 1937

Iraq Petroleum Co., Ltd., 5 July 1942

Trans-Jordan Petroleum Co., Ltd., 10 May 1947

Edwin W. Pauley Concession, 30 January 1956 (transferred to Phillips Petroleum Co.)

Phillips Petroleum Co., February 1956 (believed withdrawn)

Meurogas Holdings, Ltd., 7 June 1962

John W. Mecom, 25 March 1964

KUWAIT

Kuwait Oil Co., Ltd., 23 December 1934

American Independent Oil Co., 28 June 1948

D'Arcy Kuwait Co., Ltd., 30 December 1951

D'Arcy Kuwait Co., Ltd., Income Tax, 31 December 1951

D'Arcy Kuwait Co., Ltd., 14 May 1955

D'Arcy Kuwait Co., Ltd., Rates of Volume Discount, 14 May 1955

Arabian Oil Company, Ltd., 5 July 1958

Kuwait Shell Petroleum Development Co., Ltd., 15 January 1961

American Independent Oil Co., Supplemental, 29 July 1961

Kuwait Oil Co., Ltd., Supplemental, 17 January 1963

Kuwait Oil Co., Ltd., Natural Gas, 14 September 1963

LEBANON

Iraq Petroleum Co,. Ltd., 25 March 1931

Compagnie Française des Pétroles, 23 August 1947

Compagnie Libanaise des Pétroles, 10 August 1955

Compagnie Libanaise des Pétroles, American Group, 13 August 1957

LIBYA

In 1965 there existed in Libya 25 oil concessionaires holding, separately or jointly, various concessions in different Zones. The concessionaires were the following:

Amerada Petroleum Corp. of Libya/Continental Oil Co. of Libya/Marathon Petroleum Libya Ltd. operating through a jointly owned subsidiary named The Oasis Oil Company of Libya Inc.

Ausinia Mineraria AMI.S.p.A./D.E.A./Soc. Nationale des Pétroles d'Aquitaine

British Petroleum Exploration Co. (Libya) Ltd.

Compagnie des Pétroles Total (Libye)

Compagnia Ricerche Idrocarburi S.p.A. (CORI)

Deutsche Erdoel A.G. Libya/Wintershall A.G. Libya

Elwerath Oil Co. Libya/D.E.A./W.I.A.G.

Esso Standard Libya Inc.

Libyan American Oil Co./W. R. Grace/Esso Sirte Inc.

Gulf Oil Co. of Libya

Libyan American Oil Co./W. R. Grace

Libyan Atlantic Co./Phillips Petroleum Co. Libya

Libya Shell N.V.

Mobil Oil Libya, Ltd./Gelsenberg Benzin A.G.

Nelson Bunker Hunt

N. B. Hunt/British Petroleum Exploration Co. (Libya) Ltd.

Pan American Libya Oil Co.

Phillips Petroleum Co. Libya

Texaco Overseas Petroleum Co./California Asiatic Oil Co. operating through a jointly owned subsidiary acting as managing agent named American Overseas Petroleum Ltd. (Amoseas)

In addition, a number of new concessions were granted during the summer of 1966.

MOROCCO

BRPM (Bureau de Recherches et Participations Minières)

SCP (Société Chérifienne des Pétroles)

SOMIP

Belgian Petrofina

Preussag

Canadian Delhi Oil Co.

MUSCAT AND OMAN

Petroleum Concessions Limited, 24 June 1937

Philpryor Corporation, January 17, 1953, assigned to Cities Service Company

NEUTRAL ZONE

See under Kuwait and Saudi Arabia

OMAN

Petroleum Development (Oman), Ltd.

PALESTINE

Iraq Petroleum Co., Ltd., 5 January 1931

Iraq Petroleum Co., Ltd., 10 July 1933

Anglo-Iranian Oil Co., Ltd., 18 October 1933

Anglo-Iranian Oil Co., Ltd., Supplemental, 10 March 1938

Iraq Petroleum Co., Ltd., Supplemental, 23 September 1938

Iraq Petroleum Co., Ltd., Supplemental, 29 May 1939

PERSIA

See under Iran

QATAR

Anglo-Persian Oil Co., Ltd., 17 May 1935

Petroleum Development (Qatar), Ltd., (Convention amending Convention of 17 May 1935), 1 September 1952

Anglo-Saxon Petroleum Co., Ltd., June 1952

Shell Overseas Exploration Co., Ltd., 29 November 1952

Continental Oil Company of Qatar, Ltd., 1963

Qatar Petroleum Company, Supplemental Agreement, 31 December 1964

RAS AL KHAIMA

Kuamco Oil, S.A., 12 October 1962

SAUDI ARABIA

Eastern & General Syndicate, Ltd., 6 May 1923

Arabian American Oil Company (SOCAL), 29 May 1933

Arabian American Oil Company, Preferential Area, 29 May 1933

Petroleum Concessions, Ltd., 9 July 1936

Arabian American Oil Company, Supplemental and Letters, 31 May 1939

Arabian American Oil Company, Relinquishment)
                              Offshore Rights) 10 October
                              Neutral Zone   )   1948

Pacific Western Oil Corporation (Getty), Neutral Zone, 20 February 1949

Arabian American Oil Company, Income Tax, 30 December 1950

Arabian American Oil Company, Foreign Income Tax, 13 February 1952

Arabian American Oil Company, Increased Prices, 3 October 1954

Arabian American Oil Company, Billing Practices, 25 June 1956

Japan Petroleum Trading Co. Ltd., Neutral Zone, 10 December 1957

Arabian Oil Company, Ltd., 5 July 1958

Arabian American Oil Company, General Accounting) 24 March
                              Relinquishment   )   1963

Arabian American Oil Company, Expensing of Royalties, 25 January 1965

Société Auxiliaire de la Régie Autonome des Pétroles—AUXIRAP, 4 April 1965

Arabian American Oil Company, Third Party Discounts, 30 September 1966

SHARJAH-AJMAN

John W. Mecom and Pure Oil Company

SYRIA[2]

Iraq Petroleum Co., Ltd., 25 March 1931

---

[2] Since the end of 1964 no oil concessions can be granted in Syria.

Syria Petroleum Co., Ltd., 26 February 1938

Syria Petroleum Co., Ltd., Supplemental, 6 March 1943

Syria Petroleum Co., Ltd., Oil Loading) 27 November
Refined Products) 1955

Syria Petroleum Co., Ltd., 29 November 1955

Iraq Petroleum Co., Ltd., Supplemental, 29 November 1955

Société des Pétroles Concordia S.A.R.L., September 1956

United Petroleum Co. (Concordia) Ltd., September 1956

TUNISIA

SEREPT—Société de Recherches et d'Exploitation des Pétroles en Tunisie

BRP

Rimrock Tidelands Inc. operating for the account of a group comprising Rimrock Tidelands, Colorado Tunisia Oil, Western Tunisia Co., United Overseas Production Corp., Helis Overseas and Signal Oil

Husky Oil Company

SITEP, Société Italo-Tunisienne d'Exploitation Pétrolière, an Agip subsidiary of the ENI group

PETROPAR—Société de Participations Pétrolières

SNPA—Société Nationale des Pétroles d'Aquitaine

RAP—Régie Autonome des Pétroles

Conorada Petroleum Corp (Continental/Ohio/Amerada)

O.N.M. (Office National des Mines)

UMM QAWAIN

John W. Mecom

UNITED ARAB REPUBLIC

Eastern Petroleum Company, 5 January 1959

Phillips Petroleum Company, 25 September 1963

Pan American U.A.R. Oil Company, 23 October 1963

ENI (Compagnie Orientale des Pétroles d'Egypte), 1 December 1963

Pan American U.A.R. Oil Company, 12 February 1964

YEMEN

American Overseas Investment Corp., 1959

John W. Mecom, March 1961 (believed to cover area formerly held by American Overseas Investment).

PRODUCTION & PRODUCING AREAS IN THE MIDDLE EAST & NORTH AFRICA

CRUDE OIL PRODUCTION – 1949 VS 1965

COUNTRIES	1949		1965	
	THOUSANDS OF BARRELS	THOUSANDS OF B/D	THOUSANDS OF BARRELS	THOUSANDS OF B/D
ABU DHABI	0	0	103,660	284
ALGERIA	2	5	202,210	554
BAHRAIN	10,985	30	20,805	57
IRAN (Consortium)	204,712	561	659,920	1,808
IRAQ (I.P.C. Group)	30,957	85	478,150	1,310
KUWAIT	90,000	247	792,050	2,170
LIBYA	0	0	445,300	1,220
QATAR	750	2	70,810	194
SAUDI ARABIA (Aramco)	174,008	477	739,125	2,025
SAUDI ARABIA – KUWAIT NEUTRAL ZONE	0	0	132,130	362
UAR (EGYPT)	15,997	44	45,990	126
TOTAL	527,411	1,451	3,690,150	10,110
WORLD	3,404,132	9,326	11,035,410	29,991

Sources: 1949 data – American Petroleum Institute, Petroleum Facts and Figures, Centennial Edition 1959.

1965 data – Various Trade Publications.

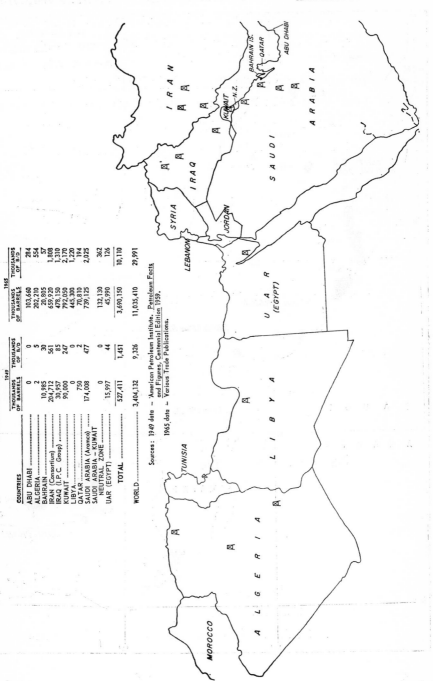

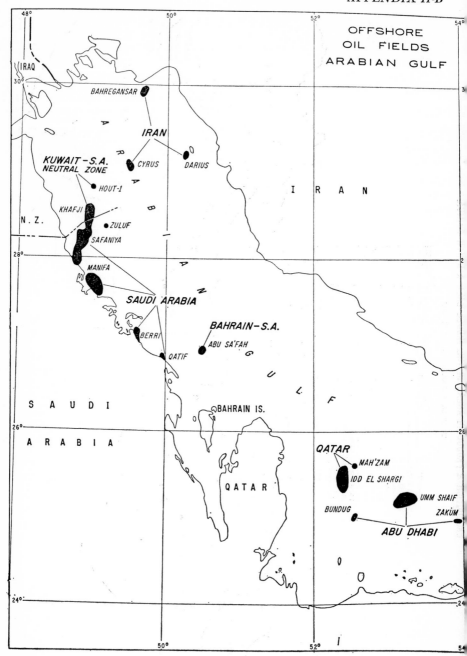

OFFSHORE
OIL FIELDS
ARABIAN GULF

APPENDIX II-C

ESTIMATED DIRECT PAYMENTS BY OIL COMPANIES TO
GOVERNMENTS IN THE MIDDLE EAST AND NORTH AFRICA
1949 AND 1964

(in millions of U. S. Dollars)

Countries	1949	1964*
Abu Dhabi	—	13
Algeria	N.A.	65
Bahrain	1	18
Iran (AIOC: Consortium)	50	480
Iraq (IPC Group)	8	353
Kuwait	12	537
Libya	—	182
Qatar (QPC only)	—	62
Saudi Arabia (Incl. Neutral Zone)	66	524
	137	2,234

Sources: 1949 data—United Nations. *Economic Developments in the Middle East, 1958-1959,* p. 77.

Payments to Saudi Arabia include $9.5 million paid by Pacific Western Oil Co.

1964 data—Abu Dhabi estimates are based on information in various trade publications.

Algeria and Libya—*Oil and Gas International,* September 1964, p. 56.

All Other Countries—The Economist Intelligence Unit, *Middle East Oil and the Arabian Peninsula, Quarterly Economic Review, Annual Supplement,* December, 1965, p. 31.

*Figures for years subsequent to 1964 not available at date of publication.

APPENDIX II-D

PROPORTION OF BUDGETED OIL REVENUE TO BUDGETED
GOVERNMENT REVENUE IN SELECTED MIDDLE EAST AND
NORTH AFRICAN COUNTRIES
(in millions of U.S. Dollars)

Countries	Estimated Total Revenue	Estimated Oil Revenue	Oil Revenue as % of Total Revenue
Bahrain (1965)	17	12	71
Iran (1964-1965)	1,204	451	37
Iraq (1964-1965)	589	310	53
Kuwait (1965-1966)	646	609	94
Libya (1965-1966)	464	347	75
Qatar (1964)	64	62	97
Saudi Arabia (1965-1966)	803	706	88

Sources: Bahrain—The Economist Intelligence Unit, *Middle East Oil and the Arabian Peninsula, Quarterly Economic Review, Annual Supplement,* December, 1965, p. 52. Oil revenues shown are those allocated directly to the State budget; the amount of oil revenues paid directly to the Ruler is not available.

Iran—The Economist Intelligence Unit, *Quarterly Economic Review, Iran,* August, 1964, pp. 4-5. Revenue estimates are those of the general budget; budgets of "organizations dependent on the Government" are excluded.

Iraq—The Economist Intelligence Unit, *Quarterly Economic Review, Annual Supplement, Iraq,* September, 1964, pp. 22-23. Estimated total revenue includes ordinary and supplementary budgets, plus 50% of estimated oil revenue allocated to development. Actual oil revenues are not available but were probably higher than the amounts estimated.

Kuwait—The Economist Intelligence Unit, *Middle East Oil and the Arabian Peninsula, Quarterly Economic Review, Annual Supplement,* December, 1965, pp. 48-49.

Libya—*Middle East Economic Survey,* August 6, 1965.

Qatar—The Economist Intelligence Unit, *Middle East Oil*

and the Arabian Peninsula, Quarterly Economic Review,
July, 1965, p. 22. Total revenues estimated.

Saudi Arabia—The Economist Intelligence Unit, *Middle
East Oil and the Arabian Peninsula, Quarterly Economic
Review,* January, 1966, p. 19. "Estimated Total Revenue"
includes new revenues only and not those transferred from
the Economic Development Fund and the general reserves.

APPENDIX II-E

WORLD RESERVES AND PRODUCTION, 1965

	Proved Reserves (end 1965)		Estimated Production (1965)	
	(million bbls)		(thousand bbls/day)	
	Quantity	Percent of Total	Quantity	Percent of Total
Middle East	215,360	61.0	8,241	27.5
Western Hemisphere	68,071	19.3	13,139	43.8
(U.S.A. only)	(35,400)	(10.0)	(7,753)	(25.9)
U.S.S.R. Bloc	33,485	9.5	5,280	17.6
Africa	23,049	6.5	2,226	7.4
Asia-Pacific	11,009	3.1	709	2.4
Europe	2,085	0.6	396	1.3
World Total	353,059	100.0	29,991	100.0

Source: *Oil and Gas International,* February 1966, pp. 42-43.

169

Fairleigh Dickinson University Library

Florham-Madison, New Jersey